Teenage Bride

Teenage Bride

A true story, written about real people, for real people.

WRITTEN AND EDITED BY
Sharon Stanford Jacobs

TEENAGE BRIDE

Copyright © Sharon Stanford Jacobs, 2024

All rights reserved. No part of this publication may be reproduced, stored in a retrieval system, or transmitted in any form or by any means, electronic, mechanical, photocopying, recording, or otherwise, without written permission of the author and publisher.

Published by Sharon Stanford Jacobs, Grimshaw, Canada

ISBN:
    Paperback   978-1-77354-608-7
        ebook   978-1-77354-609-4

Publication assistance by

PUBLISHING
PageMaster.ca

DISCLAIMER

Proper names of living people, and names of places mentioned within this book have been changed.

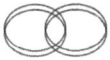

Preface

The years that it's taken to complete this book, I've learned a good deal about writing.

Firstly, writing and editing an entire manuscript is more difficult than I would have thought.

Secondly, observing the completed manuscript ready for publishing, is much more rewarding than I ever imagined it could possibly be.

From the time that first words began to formulate in my mind, for the writing of *Teenage Bride* beginning with, "She, a naïve fifteen-year-old schoolgirl, stood riveted to her spot, as she watched the tall handsome stranger descend the staircase", I knew without a doubt, that this was a story waiting to be told (excerpt from Chapter 1).

This book truly has been a labor of love. I wrote the first rough draft in less than one year. Writing is one of my greatest passions, so the original manuscript was quite effortless. It was the two drafts that followed, and the editing of the final manuscript, that took years before it was finally ready for a publisher. Once I began working on the third draft, everything slowed to a crawl. I would look at a few paragraphs or maybe a chapter, make a change or two, and set it aside. Then weeks or perhaps months could pass before I would pick it up again.

Editing of the manuscript, was even more difficult. That was actual "work", and editing is quite time consuming. I found no pleasure at all in the editing.

In fact, the final draft sat dormant for several years, waiting for me to begin the editing process. It wasn't until I decided on the title for my "next" book, that I became motivated to complete the editing work on *Teenage Bride*. Because I knew that I would not allow myself to begin writing a new manuscript until this one was finished.

When *Teenage Bride* was finally complete and ready for a publisher, and I closed my computer for the last time, knowing that my work on it was finally finished, I felt a sense of great accomplishment. It really was a feeling like no other!

Now that *Teenage Bride* is done, I will organize the mountains of notes I have compiled over the last twenty-five years that I've worked as a Prison Guard with the RCMP, and Lord willing, I will begin writing my next book: *"CELL BLOCK—My View From The Inside".*

Perhaps this time, I'll use the services of an editor, or not!

Sincerely,
Sharon Stanford Jacobs

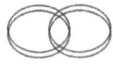

Special Thanks

- Thank you to PageMaster Publishing House in Edmonton, Alberta, for publishing my work. I am most grateful for their help in assisting me, to finally see my manuscript published.

- Thank you to Phillip Graham Jacobs, my son, who's technical computer prowess was of great benefit, when I was preparing the front and back book covers for Teenage Bride.
  While the photography work was my own, it took hours of specialized computer work to properly format the covers for my book. Again, thanks Boo!

- Thank you to Al Jacobs, my husband, in his support for me to write this book. And for his consistent encouragement for me to begin the enormous task of editing my manuscript, even after I allowed it to sit dormant for so long.

Acknowledgments of Family Who Have Most Influenced My Life:

- I acknowledge my parents: Benjamin Stanford, and Lydia Ellen Giles Stanford (Both deceased)

- I acknowledge my husband: Alvin Graham Jacobs

- I acknowledge my daughter: Tracy Maxine Jacobs Fortin (Rodney Clark Fortin)

- I acknowledge my son: Phillip Graham Jacobs (Alanna Joy Ann Oddy Jacobs)

- I acknowledge my four amazing adult Grandchildren:

    Emanuel Graham Fortin (Francine Monique Samantha Holbrook Fortin)
    Rachel Grace Ellen Fortin Dempster (Braeden John Dempster)
    Ezekiel Graham Jacobs
    Joy Lily Ann Jacobs

- I acknowledge my three precious Great-granddaughters:

  Adeline Anieka Grace Dempster
  Amadea Oriella Dempster (Deceased)
  Eliyanah Seraphina Dempster

- I acknowledge my three siblings:

  Josiah Lloyd Stanford (Deceased) (Evelyn Mable Vivian Stanford)
  Myrtle Delphine Stanford Leblanc (Stanley Lawrence LeBlanc) (Deceased)
  Maxwell Benjamin Stanford (Marcella Victoria Watton Stanford)

- I acknowledge the many others in my life, both extended family members and dear friends, whose significance to me I hold in the highest regard. I would desire to call you each by name. However, I best not, lest I unwittingly omit my dearest ones.
  You know who you are—and you know that I love and appreciate each of you.

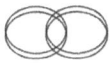

Special Acknowledgements:

- Richard & Betty Fife: Most Wise Mentors
- Joanna Twees: My Sunshine

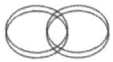

Table of Contents

1. Love At First Sight 1
2. Poor Little Rich Girl 12
3. Transportation Woes 24
4. Puppy Love 36
5. Chez Marie 41
6. Lost and Found 52
7. Here Comes the Bride 63
8. A Daughter is Born 74
9. Perception is Reality 82
10. Order in the Court 90
11. A Son is Born 102
12. The God Factor 109
13. Promises Kept 117

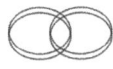

DEDICATION

I dedicate this Book to my Husband Al, My Forever Love

"Just as the Four Seasons of Nature has various unique qualities to be enjoyed—so it is, with the Seasons of a Marriage. Each new Season, is just waiting to be discovered and embraced."

Quote from the Author

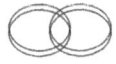

Chapter 1

Love At First Sight

She, a naïve Fifteen-year-old schoolgirl, stood riveted to her spot and watched, as Mr. tall, dark and handsome descended the open staircase towards the main floor of the Town Hall. Another young man, who was a little shorter in stature, with light colored hair followed closely behind him.

Although Shayla was being very careful not to be seen looking directly at him, she could not pull her eyes completely away, it seemed that at this moment in time, her eyes had a will of their own.

The lighting in the hall was dimmed but, not so dim that she could not appreciate how great this dark-haired stranger looked. He wore denim blue jeans and a burgundy color shirt. He had long sideburns, his dark hair that was parted on the side, was more than long enough to cover his shirt collar. His shirt buttoned up the front and horror of horrors, so did the jeans!

She had never seen jeans that buttoned up the front before. As this gorgeous stranger descended the stairs,

Shayla caught a glimpse of his eyes. It was almost like they were set on "high beam", as though he was searching the crowd for someone.

Shayla thought to herself, those two young men probably have girlfriends here who are waiting for them to arrive. Yes, that would be the reason they would be attending a junior-high school year-end party. Still, she was intrigued.

Shayla, suddenly became keenly aware of herself. Looking down, she took stock of the hot-pink sweater and the white denim jeans that she had chosen to wear and was happy enough with her choice.

Her white jeans stood out in stark contrast to the navy or black jeans the girls around her all seemed to be wearing. It appeared that, most of the other girls wore their hair either loose or cropped short. Shayla was glad that she had decided to tie her long blonde hair up in a high ponytail. She had used a black velvet hair ribbon, which had been given to her by her sister-in-law, Marsha.

Unlike most of the other girls her age, Shayla wore practically no make-up. Her face always had that fresh scrubbed appearance. Her pale skin next to the hot-pink sweater, made the natural color of her pink cheeks stand out.

Shayla, along with every other young female present in the Town Hall, had dressed for the evening with hopes that they would be asked to dance by the local boys, at least once or twice.

On this special night, most of the local youth from this small, isolated town of Burnt Harbor, were assembled for an evening of innocent partying. It was the annual celebration to mark the end of another school year.

The organizing team expected there to be about sixty or so people in attendance. That number included all the teachers as well as their escorts. This school year was an academic success for most the Town's young people. It certainly was a great success for Shayla; she had managed to accumulate some of her highest marks to date. But then, she had only just completed ninth grade. Still some time to go before Graduation.

This night had been much anticipated for quite some time because, not much exciting ever happened in Burnt Harbor. The Summers brought the occasional Wedding, which everyone attended, and then talked about or sometimes gossiped about, until the next one came along.

Shayla had worked tirelessly along with many of the other students; to ensure that the Town Hall looked it's very best for the end of the School Year event. The place really did look great, with its purple and white crepe paper decorations and matching balloons.

There were two flavors of punch, and the largest variety of sandwiches and desserts, that Shayla had ever seen. Not everyone had arrived yet and already, the DJ had begun to create a wonderful party atmosphere, by spinning records of popular songs from his extensive album collection.

The next School year, Shayla would join the other high school students that were bussed to the neighboring town of Kenwick. It was with great anticipation, she looked forward to this change of school venue. Also was the fact, that the school in Kenwick was about ten times the size of the one she attended in Burnt Harbor. This was very appealing indeed!

Shayla and her two girlfriends, Janelle and Corina were all about the same age. The three, were never terribly popular in their junior high years. They knew that to be popular, one had to do certain "things" that they were simply not willing to do.

Wearing so much make-up, that one could be mistaken for a circus clown was one of those "things." Shayla and her two friends always had a great time hanging out together—it seemed, that they never ran out of things to giggle about.

Now here they were, huddled together, just a few feet from the bottom of the stairs—watching!

It was with a very keen eye, that Shayla and her friends observed, as the two young men, who seemed to be moving in slow motion, finally reached the main floor of the hall.

Shayla had mentioned her thoughts to her friends, that the two young men likely were there to see their girlfriends—her friends agreed that this was most likely the case.

Shayla was still discretely studying the taller of the two men intently from the corner of her eye. She noticed something different about him, something almost odd. It was the "way" that he was chewing gum.

She thought, "he chews gum differently than anyone I've ever seen". Slow and deliberate, that's how he chewed his gum! It seemed, that there was something almost sensual about the process—not that Shayla would possibly know much about sensuality.

The young man that Shayla had been watching, stood at the bottom of the stairs for a few minutes talking together with his friend. During their conversation, Shayla saw him smile a couple of times. She noticed that he had a big, beautiful smile.

Then he turned, and he seemed to notice her immediately. Although she had not meant to, she was fairly certain that she had indeed made a very quick eye contact with this handsome young man. He had offered her a little smile—she blushed and quickly turned away.

Shayla's heart pounded so hard, she was sure that others could hear it. As she stood there awe-struck, she considered the possibility that maybe she had been wrong. That perhaps the two young men were not there to meet up with their girlfriends after all.

Shayla began to consider an acceptable response, in the event that "he" might ask her to dance. Suddenly Shayla felt weak, so weak she thought that she might faint dead away—she didn't!

As she endeavored to gain her composure by staring intently at her shoes, she was thinking that undoubtedly, she had just looked upon the most gorgeous young man in the entire world. By all teenage standards, he was indeed, tall, dark and handsome or, in teen-age lingo, Major Hot!

Her girlfriends seemed mesmerized and were giggling and whispering almost uncontrollably about which of the two men might ask them to dance first. Each one offered their opinions that the taller one of the two was definitely the better looking one. But, that both guys were really cute.

It was not often, that young people from other Towns ever attended a community youth event in Burnt Harbor. Now, to have not one but two, newcomers attend the year-end school event, was very much a novelty indeed.

It was clear, that most of the young girls present were very interested to have those young men ask them to dance. They were practically swooning over them. Even Shayla's two friends were not nearly as shy around boys as she was. They were looking directly at the two strangers now, giving their smiles away freely.

Shayla had essentially no experience at all with boys her own age. One of the local boys had walked her home a couple of times. He had held her hand and sneaked a kiss one time. That was about it for experience with boys her age.

But for Shayla, after just having made brief eye contact with this young stranger, she could still barely manage to lift her eyes from her feet. When she finally did look up, there "he" was—standing directly in front of her.

He had managed to make his way through the crowd and in between her girlfriends to reach her. As he looked down at her face, he smiled a wonderful smile, and speaking just above the music, he asked if she would like to have a dance with him.

She answered not a word, only placed her hand in his, which was outstretched towards her. As he led her to the dance floor for the waltz, she felt very wobbly in her knees again—this was a feeling she had never experienced before. Standing so close to him she realized how tall he was. She came up just past his shoulder so; she thought that he must be at least six feet tall.

Shayla had almost no experience with waltzing, other than the few times she had tried it with her two older brothers Wyatt and Harley. The young man, who now held her in his arms, did not seem to mind the fact that, during that first waltz, she stepped on his toes too many times to count.

The young man, who was no longer a total stranger, told Shayla that his name was Calvin, that he was eighteen, and that he and his friend Ron were from a place called Morristown, which was just over an hour's drive away. The fact that, he had asked her to dance before any other girl, only made it all the sweeter for Shayla.

From the dance floor, she could see many of the other girls watching, and they looked green with envy. Much to Shayla's delight, it appeared that all the "popular" girls were just a little more "green" than the others.

The fact that Calvin's friend Ron, had asked one of the girls on the other side of the room to dance, only added to the frustrating stares directed towards Shayla. As the waltz came to a finish, Shayla was certain that Calvin would move on to dance with other girls.

As was often the case at social events, the number of girls outnumbered that of guys by at least two-to-one. Calvin and

Ron would likely dance with a different girl for each dance of the evening. With their looks and charm, the two young men would certainly have their choice of dance partners.

After their waltz, Calvin led Shayla back to her two friends, where he had first found her. She was surprised that he did not move away from her—he just stood there beside her. What's more, he still hadn't released her hand. She was embarrassed and simply did not know how to respond. This was brand new territory for Shayla.

After standing there rather awkwardly for a couple of minutes, Shayla gathered her thoughts and finally introduced Calvin to Corina and Janelle. Then, another surprise, Calvin asked her if she would like to accompany him to the snack table for a glass of punch and a snack. Shayla smiled and nodded yes.

After enjoying a couple of snacks and some punch, Calvin asked if she would like to dance some more. She said yes that she absolutely loved dancing. Away the two of them went towards the dance floor once again. Under the very watchful eye of the school Principal and Teachers, Shayla and Calvin danced together on the crowded dance floor for several more songs.

Then Calvin suggested that maybe they could join some of the others outside on the veranda. He said it might be easier to talk out there where it would be quieter.

They went and found Corina and Janelle over beside the snack table and told them that they would be just outside on the veranda for a few minutes. Shayla invited her friends to join them on the veranda, saying there were lots of other people out there. But Janelle and Corina declined. Shayla was glad.

Shayla and Calvin made their way through the crowd and out onto the veranda, into the cool breeze of the beautiful summer evening. Calvin told Shayla that he would very much like to see her again sometime if she would be interested. Shayla said that she would quite like that.

He went on to say that he was saving up money to buy his first car, but that it would still be a while before he'd be able to buy one. He explained that his current form of transportation was hitch-hiking. Or sometimes arranging a ride with someone.

This was exactly what Calvin and Ron had done that evening. Calvin knew someone from his hometown who had a fiancé who lived in Burnt Harbor. So, he and Ron was travelling both directions with him that evening. After about a half hour talking and laughing together on the veranda, they went back inside, where they danced together the entire rest of the evening.

It was almost eleven o'clock and the evening's festivities were winding down, when Calvin quietly asked Shayla, "will you do me a favor"? Shayla nodded and said, "If I can". He asked her "Would you mind removing the ribbon from your hair? I would love to see your hair frame your face".

She blushed and smiled at him and then she whispered barely loud enough for him to hear, "It is tied up in a simple bow. Why don't you do it?". Before Shayla had time to change her mind, Calvin reached up and very gently released the black velvet ribbon from her hair. He stepped back just a little and watched, as her straight blond hair tumbled down her shoulders reaching nearly to her waist.

The expression on his face told Shayla that he was well pleased with the picture. Shayla did not notice at the time but, instead of giving her the hair ribbon, he scrunched it in his hand and discretely shoved it into the pocket of his jeans.

Focusing back on the waltz that would be the last one of the evening, he looked deep into her eyes and said, "I feel that I would like to dance with "only" you for the rest of my life. I have never believed in love at first sight, but I felt something different, when I first saw you here tonight. I understand if that may sound a bit cheesy to you".

Calvin also said that, looking at her, reminded him of a Country song that he really liked. Then he asked her if she had ever heard Anne Murray's country song entitled, "Could I have this dance for the rest of my life?" He went on to whisper the first verse of the waltz into her ear—"Could I have this dance for the rest of my life? Would you be my partner, every night? When we're together, it seems so right, could I have this dance, for the rest of my life?"

Shayla replied that not only had she heard of the song, but that it was one of her very favorites. Calvin then led the way over to the stage where the DJ was standing and requested the song to be played. The DJ agreed to do one more final song by special request. As the song began to play, Calvin held Shayla tightly in his arms, and he kissed her then, completely and soundly, right on the mouth and she liked it—a lot!

After the kiss that neither one of them would ever forget, it was time to say goodnight. After exchanging phone numbers, and waving goodbye, Calvin and his friend Ron were gone. Both him and Shayla felt a sense of contentment to be alone with their thoughts, to consider the events of the evening.

As Shayla and her two girlfriends made their way home, she smiled to herself, as she pondered memories from the marvelous evening she'd just had with this extraordinary young man. Shayla knew in her heart she would be seeing him again, very soon.

As Calvin and Ron rode along on the drive back to their hometown that night, Calvin couldn't keep from smiling. He thought to himself, what was That? This young lady named Shayla had captivated him. He wasn't sure if maybe he just had a big crush on her, or if possibly it might have been "love at first sight".

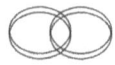

Chapter 2

Poor Little Rich Girl

Shayla was born the second daughter and last of four children, to her parents Lydia and Benjamin. Her pending birth came as a very great surprise—some might even say "shock" to her family. Her siblings, Harley, Jaclyn, and Wyatt were twelve, eleven and ten years older respectively.

For all intent and purposes, Shayla was raised like an only child. She was treated special not only by her parents, but by her three siblings also. As special as she was always made to feel, unfortunately, Shayla was raised without any sort of discipline.

She did exactly what she wanted, exactly when she wanted. Shayla, even at the young age of six or seven years, certainly appeared to run things as she pleased, in the big old two-story family home.

Night after night, Shayla would go upstairs, and instead of going to bed, she would play imaginary games all alone for hours. One of her favorite games, was to walk quietly across the covered wooden planks of the floor and listen to the squeaks and groans of the floorboards. It seemed they always had something different to say. She even tried to make a musical tune out of the sounds. Shayla seemed to develop a great imagination at a very early age.

Shayla was a personable child, well-liked by friends and neighbors alike. In fact, the next-door neighbors—the Renolds family loved Shayla. And she absolutely adored the entire Renolds family. There were two brothers who had houses next door to each other. They each had their own family. Shayla spent a tremendous amount of time at their homes when she was a child—she often ate meals there.

When the grandfather Renolds passed away, the grandma became grief-stricken for an extended period of time. It seemed only Shayla could cheer her up. Shayla was like one of the family, and they completely spoiled her. Especially at Christmas time or during her birthday. Shayla always had a Christmas stocking stuffed to overflowing at the Renolds house, as well as the one at her own family home. Not to mention a mountain of Christmas gifts. Shayla was a very privileged child.

By most accounts, Shayla's Family was rather poor. This was because her father was sick for years, and unable to work. Although there seemed to be very little money, there always seemed to be plenty available when Shayla needed or wanted something.

When Shayla was in the third grade, her mom Lydia, set up charge accounts for her at both shops where Shayla frequented in their hometown. Joey's Grocery, which was located a two-minute walk from her middle school, and Renolds Confectionary, that one was just a five minute walk from her home.

There was no limit to "how much" she could charge to the store accounts; in fact, the subject of "amount" was never mentioned. Shayla's mom simply informed her that she could go there and "buy" whatever she wanted.

Amazingly enough, Shayla never once took advantage by giving things away to others at her Parents expense. She purchased only the items that she wanted for herself. She would then share those things with her friends. Shayla was always a very generous child. Never selfish.

Her mom also set up an account through the mail-order catalogue. This was used to purchase Shayla's clothes, footwear and the like. Though her family seemed poor, she was indeed raised very much like a spoiled little rich girl.

As a child, Shayla had several friends her age, but she would just as soon play alone. She was her own best friend. During those early, formative years, Shayla spent much of her time alone, or with adults.

She was also a very avid reader. She read everything she got her hands on, including the men's magazines she "found" in her brothers' bedroom. She possessed an amazing imagination and had an insatiable appetite to learn new things about the world around her. All of these were contributing factors, which seemed to make Shayla mature beyond her years.

Also contributing to early maturity was the fact that, by the time She was about fourteen years old, Shayla had been molested by two different men in their twenties and thirties, respectively.

No rape occurred. No sexual intercourse occurred. However, both men, who were well known to Shayla, had molested, and sexually interfered with her many, many times.

The first abuse situation happened when she was about twelve. She was visiting her sister Jaclyn in the city for summer vacation. Often, while at work, Jaclyn's boyfriend would find a "reason" to stop by her apartment, knowing that Shayla would be there alone.

Shayla was not the first child he had molested. He had an album of polaroid photos of the children and teenagers that he kept as a trophy. Shayla knew this to be true, because he showed her the album, which contained photos of about a dozen different minor children, posing nude or semi-nude in various poses for his camera.

After showing her the album, he tried desperately hard to convince Shayla to become the next "special princess" for his photo album. Each time he came over, he brought his polaroid camera inside a black zippered bag.

This bag also contained various other items; Besides the special treats he always brought for Shayla, all the other items were special things he used for the photo sessions—a white shawl made of feathers, a red sheer cape, a small kit of make-up, which he liked to apply to the faces of his "Princesses".

There was also a small tiara. He had explained that the tiara was reserved for his most special Princesses. Only those who complied with all his desires got to wear the tiara for special photos. Shayla had noticed the tiara worn in some of the photos.

Shayla never did allow him to photograph her without clothing.

The abuse from that pedophile finally ended very abruptly one day, when the older lady who lived one floor below, heard Shayla scream at him to Stop. A moment later the door swung wide open, and the lady observed him in a state of partial undress. The lady said to him very sternly, "You'd best be leaving now!"

He left immediately. Shayla never saw him ever again.

Jaclyn was not told that she was dating a pedophile. A few Years later, Shayla heard that he had married, and shortly thereafter, died in an accident.

The second situation of molestation and sexual interference began about two Years after the first. It was a very difficult situation. And was complicated by the fact that this man was a non-blood relative of Shayla.

Once Shayla was able to situate herself, whereby he no longer had access to her, the abuse stopped. However, when Shayla would see him, he continued to aggravate the situation by telling her in less eloquent words, that what happened between them, would "always be their little secret". Because he knew that Shayla would never reveal his affections towards her, because she knew how such information would hurt the family.

He was correct!

Shayla later came to understand, that both of those men, as with all pedophiles, had many things in common. They preyed upon her because she was very young and vulnerable. They were monsters!

They deserved to have been charged with numerous criminal offences. Not the least of which were: Sexual interference of a minor; Molestation; Sexual harassment; And Child pornography.

No charges were ever laid, because Shayla told no one of the things that had happened to her.

For some young girls, enduring such abuse from two men that she knew, especially a relative, might have turned them off from men altogether, but not Shayla. She knew that all men were certainly not like those two perverts. Even at that young age, Shayla realized she had already seen firsthand, some of the worst of humanity. She would find a way to move past it.

It was around the time of the first incident, when Shayla was about twelve, that her father Benjamin died at the age of sixty-one. His death was the result of a lengthy illness of hypertension. This illness, otherwise known as high blood pressure, often causes people to have strokes. Stroke is defined as lack of oxygen reaching the brain.

Shayla's Dad had suffered many such strokes. Which often left him incapacitated to various degrees. Often, the result of a stroke would deform his facial features and cause him to be paralyzed on one or both sides of his body.

Other times, it would be only one arm, or one leg affected. The suddenness of the stroke would usually cause him to fall to the floor, whether he had been standing or sitting at the time. He could suffer a stroke several times in any given week, or only once in six months. The paralysis sometimes lasted for weeks. One month before his death, he was moved to the Hospital.

One night, as the family slept, the dreaded, but expected phone call came from the Hospital with the news that her dad had passed away. Shayla was astonished by the fact that her immediate reaction to this news was that of relief, followed by shame.

She had previously often wondered and obsessed about just how she would feel when that news would come. But she had never considered that she would feel those emotions. It had been known for years, that because of the illness, her dad's time on earth would be short.

Shayla later realized that the reason she felt shame at hearing this news, was because the only real emotion she was experiencing at her dad's passing, was one of tremendous relief. She kept her feelings to herself, just as she always had—Shayla had become very good at that.

Many Years later, Shayla would come to realize that the reason she felt relief at her dad's passing, was because she had endured extreme emotional trauma, by being left alone in the family home so often with him when he was so very sick, when she was extremely young.

With Shayla's three siblings so much older than herself, they had long moved out of the family home, this left only Shayla, her mom and her very ill father in the family home.

In the final half dozen Years of her father's life, when Shayla was between six and twelve, Shayla's mom Lydia seemed to be heavy burdened in caring for such a sickly Husband, it seemed she often needed to get away from the pressure.

Even on his best days, Benjamin was very sick and could do little for himself. So, for a break, Lydia would often go visiting a friend, or to her lady's meetings. Usually, two or three evenings each week she would go out, after the evening meal was finished.

The great problem with Lydia leaving the family home so frequently was, she would leave Shayla at home alone with a dad who could at any moment, drop to the floor from a stroke and become deformed or worse—die! On numerous occasions, Shayla told her mom that she didn't like being at home alone with her dad, that it made her very scared that he might die. Her concerns were dismissed.

For all those times alone with her father, Shayla had a system. A system that no one else knew about. First, she would make sure that the neighbors phone number was next to the telephone, in case something terrible happened to her dad. Next, she would bring the small wind-up clock and place it on the floor in front of her, so she could watch for the time when her mom was expected to return home—Lydia usually returned on time.

Finally, Shayla would sit herself down, holding on tightly to both sides of her chair, directly across from her father, and as he watched the television screen, as he usually did, Shayla would watch him. She would watch him so intently for signs of a stroke, that she would often forget to breathe.

Many times, she became dizzy and almost blacked out due to not breathing. Her arms would become very tired, because she held them straight, as she held tightly to her chair. From the time that her mother would leave until her return, Shayla felt completely terrified at the thought of being alone in the house with her sick father. In fact, she often had terrible nightmares about her dad dying while in her care.

Over the Years, Shayla's worst nightmare came to pass on five or six separate occasions. Alone, in the evening time with her dad, she watched in utter horror as he suffered debilitating, deforming strokes after falling to the floor. She always tried to catch him, to prevent him from falling and injuring himself, but she wasn't strong enough, and she too would fall under his weight.

There were a couple of times Shayla sustained minor injuries from the weight of her dad falling on her. The first time Shayla recalls her father suffering a stroke while in her care, was when She was about seven years old, and it was Wintertime.

Her dad slid right of his chair unto the floor and curled up into the fetal position. When Shayla finally managed to get her feet to move, she was so terrified that, she forgot all about phoning the Renolds house for help. Instead, she ran through the snow to the neighbor's house—without a jacket in subzero temperatures.

Her Father's illness affected her to such a degree that even while in class at school, when the office phone would ring, Shayla would nearly jump out of her skin. Thinking her dad had suffered another stroke and died. Her constant confusion was, she couldn't decide whether his death would be good news or bad news.

It would be many Years after his passing, that Shayla would be able to cry a tear for the loss of her father. And even more Years after that, before she had a discussion with her mother, about the terrible decision she had made in leaving Shayla alone so frequently to care for her sick father. Especially, at such a young age.

Lydia felt mortified at the childhood trauma she had caused her young daughter. She explained, that at the time, she had felt completely overwhelmed with caring for her deathly sick Husband and a young child. She said sometimes, she felt like she was losing her mind. Shayla choose to believe that her mother did the best she could with the tools she had at the time and forgave her.

After her father's death, it seemed that her mother tried to make up for the loss in Shayla's life with even more material possessions. Lydia had meant well and expressed love for her youngest child by buying her everything under the sun. But the thing that Shayla craved most in the World, was a healthy balanced life.

Her Sister and Brothers also favored her with all sorts of material possessions. Shayla would tear pages from the mail order catalogue, with preferred items circled, with gift ideas for up-coming birthday or Christmas presents.

With her choices made, Shayla would post mail the pages to her sister who was living in Toronto. Jaclyn never disappointed her—not one time. In fact, Shayla usually received many or all of her preferred items from her sister.

Wyatt, the youngest of Shayla's two brothers, would come home after being away working, he would give her all the pocket coins that he had saved up for her while away. This usually amounted to many dollars. He would also arrive with special treats for Shayla whenever he was away.

Although he didn't know it, Wyatt was Shayla's protector when she was small. Whenever she was bullied in the Schoolyard, or by a certain School teacher, which did happen one time, she would threaten to tell Wyatt, the bullying would immediately stop!

Harley, her oldest Brother, would lavish her with presents for no special occasion at all. Shayla's bounty from one of Harley's shopping trips consisted of a new pair of figure skates, a toboggan, and a fancy new jacket, in the color that he knew she favored. She was ecstatic with joy—any child would be.

Near the family home, there was a fenced area that had once been used as a garden. Harley took away part of the fence, drove his new Volkswagen Beetle car inside, and allowed Shayla to learn to drive it while propped up on books—just because she wanted to.

Shayla thought all of this was wonderful. Every kid's dream is to have everything they ever ask for—and then some. Shayla dearly loved being the baby of the family.

The most intellectual minds in the world, could never conceive a more effective plan to ensure that a child would grow up to be completely out of touch with reality.

As future Years would continue to unfold the story of Shayla's young adult life, the incredible trauma and imbalance of her early Years, would become a very great stumbling block for her.

Life would soon become a sobering reality for Shayla, who never had to work, cook, clean, do laundry, or anything for herself—ever!

As a child and preteen, everything she wanted was hers for the asking. Shayla "was" indeed, very much like a poor little rich girl.

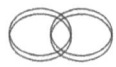

Chapter 3

Transportation Woes

Each week, usually on Friday, Calvin would manage to hitch a ride the fifty or so miles from his home in Morristown to Burnt Harbor, where his sweetheart Shayla lived. Since he did not yet own a vehicle, hitchhiking was his only form of transportation. Come rain, snow, hail, sunshine or all the above, Calvin seldom ever missed a Friday.

Hitchhiking was a very common source of transportation back in those days. Especially for guys. Girls almost never hitchhiked. Certainly, Shayla never did. Almost never, would a vehicle pass by a hitchhiker without stopping to see where he was going. However, still there had to "be" traffic on the roads for hitchhiking to be successful.

Calvin would arrive in Burnt Harbor, usually late afternoon or very early evening, go to his friend's home, where he would phone Shayla and then they would meet up. That was long before the days of cell phones. They would often go to the Town's youth hangout.

At the hang-out, they would play pinball or pool. Calvin always had money to buy snacks for them to share. Shayla always had money with her as well, but Calvin would never allow her to pay for anything. She did not yet realize that this was a characteristic of the true gentleman that Calvin was.

Calvin was already finished High School. He had graduated earlier that same year. Though, he was working at a nearby shipyard, he earned very little. It was a job that offered no real future. During this time, having gotten to know Shayla better, Calvin was for the first time, really beginning to consider his future, and his earning ability, or lack thereof.

When weather permitted, the two sweethearts would walk for miles and miles on the dusty unpaved roads of Burnt Harbor. It was during those long walks, that they would talk about the future that, after six months of dating, they had claimed as their own. They would even sometimes speak about the "one-day", when they would marry.

After an evening together, Calvin would walk Shayla home. They were always very careful never to allow Shayla's mom Lydia to see them together. Her mom did not know about Calvin, not that she wouldn't have approved of Calvin, she simply would not have approved of Shayla dating "anyone". Especially a boy who was nearly four years older. Shayla's mom felt strongly that fifteen Years of age, was much too young to date. Most people agreed.

Calvin always kissed Shayla goodbye, and she loved his kisses. But she loved his "hello" kisses even more. For, when they said good-bye, she would always be so very sad. Knowing it would be at least a Week before seeing her sweetheart again.

Shayla would feel sad as she watched him, from the living room window of her home, as he would walk the half kilometer up the hill to the main road, where he would hitch a ride back to Morristown. The telephone was a very useful tool for the two young sweethearts, during the early months of their relationship—they would talk for hours on end.

On the evenings that they were together, they made sure that they always said good-bye in good time for Calvin to catch the traffic back to his hometown. They were always very conscious of this, particularly during winter months—well, almost always!

One frigid January night, Calvin stayed a little too late before leaving to hitch a ride back home and by then, traffic was scarce. They were both a little concerned when they realized the lateness of the hour. Shayla was relieved when she saw a truck stop at the top of the hill where Calvin stood with his thumb held out. She watched as he hopped inside the vehicle for his ride home.

Shayla later discovered, the driver of the truck had told Calvin that he was going only about half-way, and that he would be turning in the opposite direction at the next intersection. He had asked Calvin, if he was sure that he wanted to take the chance of getting stuck out in the middle of no-where on such a bitterly cold night, with temperatures expected to drop to well below zero.

Calvin felt an assurance, that since this driver was out on the road, there would surely be other vehicles out also. After all, it was only about ten o'clock, and he was wearing a very warm parka, boots and mittens. So, Calvin thanked the driver for his concern and assured him that he would be fine.

As they drove along, Calvin and the driver enjoyed some good conversation and then at the appointed intersection, the truck came to a stop and Calvin said thanks and goodbye to the kindly gentleman who had given him the lift.

As Calvin stood beside the roadway, he watched the taillights of the old pick-up truck as they faded into the darkness of the night. The temperature had dipped lower. Even for January, it seemed colder than usual.

After walking on, in the direction of his home for what seemed like forever, but probably not more than an hour, Calvin realized that he had a very big problem on his hands. Looking at his wristwatch, but unable to read the time due to the darkness, he conceded to himself that there would likely be no more vehicles coming that way for the rest of the night.

Calvin seriously began to consider his options. He began to look around for some sort of shelter from the glacial wind that seemed to have whipped up from out of no-were. After walking on for a while longer, he spotted what he thought to be the outline of a small building of some sort, just a short distance ahead.

After making his way to the building, he found that the wind had drifted the snow halfway up the door. Once he managed to reach the door through all the snow, he found the sizable padlock on the door to be very secure.

He also found a very large sign on the building that informed him that this was the regional building used by Canada Post, which supplied mail for all the surrounding Towns in the general area.

Try as he might, there was no way to get that door open. Realizing defeat, Calvin took shelter from the bitter cold wind behind the wooden building. Standing there, he realized that he could no longer feel his toes, and his fingers were also beginning to lose sensation. He knew that he would have to try to start a small fire to keep from freezing to death.

From behind the small building where he was sheltering himself, he moved a safe distance away, gathered whatever small wood pieces he could find for kindling, and using a bic lighter he pulled from his pocket, he started a small fire.

Dry kindling was at a definite minimum because everything was covered in a foot of snow. With a small fire now burning, the glow from it was a stark contrast to the blackness of the night. The warmth from the fire was a very welcome sensation indeed.

Besides the few pieces of kindling, Calvin had also foraged and found a small piece of plastic underneath the shack, this he placed on the ground to separate himself from the snow as he sat down warming himself beside the small fire.

As he now settled down, Calvin wondered how many hours he would be waiting before morning traffic would start rumbling down the bumpy, snowy road. It was on that night, that Calvin learned for the first time, what being alone "really" felt like. He was later heard to say, "that the stillness of that cold moonless night was so intense, that is was like a great loud noise roaring in his ears."

Very soon, the kindling that Calvin had managed to locate was all burnt, and the fire was quickly fading. Anxious to see the time, he moved closer to the dying embers to see his wristwatch. As he pushed up his parka sleeve and pulled his heavy mitten down enough to see the time, a smile appeared on Calvin's face.

It was not the actual "time" that he was smiling about, he was smiling at the huge "S" he had etched in the crystal of his watch a few weeks earlier. He had done this using the tip of a sharp instrument, on one after-noon when he was particularly missing Shayla.

Suddenly Calvin no longer felt alone and lonely. With wonderful thoughts and memories of Shayla flooding his mind and warming his heart, he suddenly felt rejuvenated. After checking the time of night and found it to be just past two am, he realized that if he ever was to see Shayla's sweet smile again, he would need to find more kindling and quickly.

He searched and searched. There was nothing to be found that could be used for kindling—everything was either wet or buried beneath the snow.

The shack had a small space underneath it on the one side. So, Calvin dug through the snow and crawled in as far as possible. He managed to find a few small sticks of dry wood as well as two more pieces of plastic.

This was good, although it was nowhere enough kindling to see him through the night, he hoped it would be enough to keep him from freezing, until the traffic began to start moving again. Which, by his estimate, should happen in about four hours.

While getting himself back and re-kindling the fire, Calvin noticed that on the back of the building, there were some pieces of wood siding that looked less secure than the rest. Calvin knew full well that this mail house was the property of the Canadian Government and that, if anyone was found to damage it in any way, there would likely be serious consequences to follow.

Still, he went back and using his lighter, he looked again at the boards attached to the lower back wall of the building. He figured if it were a choice between freezing to death and defacing Government Property—he would choose to live.

He reasoned within himself, that if he ever had to answer for his actions of this night, he would use that as his defense—that he chose "life over death".

It was decided, he would pull of any boards that he found to be loose. And in so doing, he would hopefully have enough kindling to see him through the night. The building stood a good three feet taller than Calvin's six feet. So hopefully, there would be a good supply of loose wallboards to choose from.

He worked tirelessly, pulling off one piece of board after the other. In fact, he had worked up quite a sweat. He had to unzip his outer parka. After about thirty minutes, he had what he thought to be enough wood to see him through. He looked at the pile of wood that he had accumulated and felt pleased with his decision and satisfied with his efforts.

Now suddenly, he felt extremely tired and wanted to rest. After breaking the lengths of the whitewashed boards in half, Calvin placed a few pieces on the fire, just enough to keep a small flame going. Then he stretched the pieces of plastic out on the snow, close enough to the fire for warmth. And there, after zipping his parka back up again, he lay down to rest, and hopefully sleep a little.

He was not certain what it was that awakened him, whether it was his uncomfortable bed or the intense heat. Whatever it was, Calvin sat bolt upright.

The small fire that had been burning when he had drifted off to sleep had become a much larger fire. In fact, the fire had somehow spread to the pile of boards he had for kindling a few feet away, and onto the Canada Post mail house.

The back of the building was now on fire. Totally panic stricken, Calvin jumped up, pulling off his parka, he grabbed a couple of wood pieces, and began feverishly to shovel snow upon the burning building. Which by now, had flames reaching quarter of the way up.

After what seemed like an eternity, the flames on the building were finally extinguished. From what he could see, the fire had not burnt through the inside wall, but about half of the back side of the shack was charred black. The part of the back wall that had not burned, was so blackened with smoke that it looked as bad as the rest.

This was not good! Calvin thought "How had this night gone so wrong"?

Completely exhausted, he fell back down onto his makeshift bed. He felt too tired to even get up to find his parka. Although, he knew he would have to, due to the very cold temperature. So, it was with very great effort that Calvin got up and retrieved his parka from the snowbank where it had landed, on the other side of the fire. He put it back on, zipped and tied it up so tight that he could barely see out the hood.

He sat back down and checked the time once again. By then, it was nearly five am. He would not allow himself to sleep anymore, not that he could anyway. Not after that horrifying nightmare with the fire.

It would be light soon, and traffic would resume. Taking people, who had just spent a comfortable, normal night sleeping in their warm bed, to their workplaces, shopping or wherever. Calvin longed for his own bed—never again would he complain that the mattress was too soft. Or, about the fact that he had to share the room with his brother.

As the light of a new day dawned, there was still a significant amount of smoke emulating from the backside of the Canada Post mail building. Now, instead of wishing for traffic to hurry and come along to take him home, Calvin was very concerned about the smoke.

If someone noticed it, there would be questions asked, the authorities would be called—Calvin was very worried as he began to wonder if this nightmare would ever end. He also wondered to himself, "whether this would be the worst day of his life!"

There was almost no smoke left to be seen when the first vehicle came by at nearly seven-thirty that morning. It was headed in the opposite direction of where Calvin needed to go anyway.

For safety's sake, Calvin hid in the bushes, just in case the occupants in the car did notice smoke and decide to check it out. He did not want to be found anywhere near where a Government building had been defaced and partially burned.

Since the vehicle did not stop, Calvin assumed that they had not noticed any smoke—although, there was still a small amount slowly wafting up into the early morning clouds. Soon after the first car passed by, Calvin could hear another one coming. And this one was headed in the direction of Morristown.

Before the car came into sight, Calvin quickly jumped from the bushes and stuck out his thumb. The car stopped and Calvin jumped in. The driver turned out to be someone from Calvin's own hometown, which was very convenient.

Calvin didn't talk much on the ride home that morning. He only answered a couple of questions regarding why he smelled of smoke, and why he looked like he hadn't slept in a week. Calvin's reply to both of those questions could not be considered anywhere close to being truthful.

Soon enough, Calvin was dropped off beside his family home. After proper thanks was given to the driver, Calvin went inside his Family home. He was pleased to see that his parents and siblings were still sleeping, because he really did not feel like being on the receiving end of twenty questions. The first of which would be, where he had spent the night?

While the hot pulsing water from the shower poured down over him, Calvin began to consider all that had happened. He decided that it might be in his best interest to not tell anyone, about the events of the previous night— except for Shayla of course. He also began to realize how close he had come to freezing to death.

After pondering his transportation situation, he realized that he would have to make some changes. He decided that he would phone Shayla later that day and explain that unless he had a confirmed ride both directions—which sometimes happened, he would have to wait for warmer temperatures before he would venture hitchhiking over to Burnt Harbor again.

While he knew it would be extremely difficult to stay away from seeing her, he decided that, for safety sake, there would be no more sub-zero hitchhiking ventures for him. He felt totally confidant that Shayla would understand. In fact, he knew that she would want it that way.

She had always been very concerned about him hitching rides in the cold winter conditions. Feeling completely content with his decisions, Calvin finished his shower and went immediately to his room and with a great sigh of complete exhaustion, he fell into bed and slept soundly on his too-soft mattress which, on that day, felt perfect!

The windshield wipers on the big rig truck were working at a rapid pace, trying to keep the windshield clear of snow. Which, due to the extreme cold temperature, was quickly turning to ice. The driver could see through the falling snow, a hitchhiker bundled up in a parka with his mittened thumb stuck out beckoning for a ride.

The driver thought to himself, "Why on earth would anyone be hitching a ride on an afternoon like this?" The tractor-trailer was grinding loudly, as the driver geared down to a full stop. Turning his window down, the driver said, "Jump in—where are you headed on such a cold, snowy day? Wherever it is, it must be pretty important". As Calvin hopped up into the cab of the semi, he answered, "Yes, it is important...you see sir, it's been six days now, since I last saw my sweetheart in Burnt Harbor!".

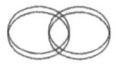

Chapter 4

Puppy Love

It was at the very beginning of what was to be a long and cold Winter, that the song "Puppy Love" was released by the Beatles. It went on to become the most popular song of the year.

It was around that same time, that most of Calvin and Shayla's families first became aware of their romance. The two had first met and began dating in June of the previous year, and by then; it was nearing the end of February—Eight months!

It was also about that same time that Shayla and Calvin come to realize with certainty, that they absolutely wanted to marry. So, from that time forward, every plan they made, was with that express purpose in mind.

At that point, the two sweethearts were not sexually active, they had only physically gone to "second base" as it was called. Calvin had never pressured Shayla regarding sex, but she knew that it would be only a matter of time before they would advance their level of intimacy. She had told Calvin that they would not become fully intimate until they became engaged. He was perfectly fine with that.

Without telling Calvin, Shayla had decided that when they were nearing the time of becoming engaged, she would begin taking birth control pills. She was never an individual who liked surprises much, not even pleasant ones.

Shayla was an organized person and liked things to be well planned as much as possible. So, a future unplanned pregnancy was something Shayla would be very careful to prevent. Besides, the two of them had decided that once married, they wanted to wait at least two years, before starting a family.

For a young couple to be together eight months and not be fully intimate, was definitely a rarity. Unless they were Christian couples. In which case, they would be expected to abstain until after marriage. Calvin and Shayla certainly were not a Christian couple. Neither one had any real knowledge of God. But they did manage to exercise a good deal of self-control.

This popular song entitled "Puppy Love", seemed to epitomize the degree of significance that some family members showed concerning Calvin and Shayla's relationship. "It won't last. It's just puppy love", some of them were heard to say.

However, the lack of enthusiasm from family members did not discourage Calvin and Shayla. They continued to see each other whenever possible, and otherwise burn up the telephone lines. This was the first serious relationship for Calvin, and the first relationship of any sort for Shayla.

It was Shayla's older Sister Jaclyn, who first showed any encouragement regarding the relationship of her younger Sister and her new "friend". Shayla had shared a little with Jaclyn, about her feelings for Calvin.

She also shared with Jaclyn how she wished that, she could tell their mom Lydia, about Calvin, and to maybe have him come to their house on occasion. Even after all these Months, Shayla had never once mentioned Calvin to her mom, she knew intuitively that her mom would never allow it. Her mother had always said that she was too young to date.

One weekend, when Shayla's Sister Jaclyn and her husband Trevor were home from the city for a visit, something happened that would change the immediate course of Shayla and Calvin's relationship.

Shayla was awaiting Calvin's phone call, and when the phone rang, Jaclyn beat her to it, and answered the phone. She introduced herself as Shayla's older Sister, and promptly invited Calvin over to the house. With some fear and trepidation, Calvin accepted the invitation.

Jaclyn hung up the phone and said "Mom, that was Shayla's friend Calvin on the phone, and I invited him over here to meet us. He's at a neighbor's house and will be here in about five minutes".

Just as Shayla had predicted, her mom threw a hissy fit and said, "Well, this guy might be coming over to our house, but he won't be meeting me". As Lydia grabbed her jacket and bolted for the door, over her shoulder she said, "I'll be down at my friend's house".

Just as Lydia pulled the front door open to leave, Calvin nearly fell into the porch, while desperately trying to avoid a collision with the lady he knew would be none other than, Shayla's mother.

Lydia sidestepped Calvin, and just kept right on going. She was moving so fast, she probably could not have stopped even if she had wanted to, which she certainly did not.

Shayla was mortified—she didn't know how to respond, whether to laugh or to cry. Besides her own emotions, she was totally and completely embarrassed for Calvin, who by now was the color of a very ripe tomato.

Jaclyn was very pleasant and tried to make light of the awkward situation. She seemed genuinely happy to meet Calvin, as was the case with Trevor. In fact, after a short time visiting, Jaclyn and Trevor suggested that they all drive to the next town, where they knew of a restaurant where they could all have an early dinner—their treat.

Shayla and Calvin were happy for the diversion, thinking that their comfort level might be enhanced if they could get on neutral turf. The time spent with Jaclyn & Trevor was indeed very pleasant, and the four of them had a nice time together. Calvin was his usual charming self, the entire time.

Jaclyn later suggested to her mom that she ought to meet this young man that Shayla was spending so much time with. She also suggested that the family might do well to begin taking this relationship seriously. Shayla had always been grateful for her older sister, but never so grateful as on that day.

Finally, her relationship with Calvin had been given some legitimacy and a degree of acceptance. And so it was, that the whole unpleasant episode of Calvin coming to meet some of Shayla's family on that fateful evening, was the beginning of great change for Shayla and Calvin's relationship—a definite change for the better. Perhaps finally, Calvin and Shayla's relationship would no longer be synonymous with the song, "Puppy Love".

After some time passed, Shayla's mom did come to accept the fact that her young daughter was in a serious relationship with this young man named Calvin. Lydia had not only come to accept that fact but, over the months that followed, she had indeed come to like Calvin very much.

In fact, when Calvin would come to see Shayla at her house for a visit or for supper, Lydia would get a hug from Calvin before Shayla did.

It was just a short time after first meeting Shayla's mom, Calvin also had occasion to meet her two brothers. Harley and Wyatt both felt that Shayla was too young to be seriously seeing anyone. Especially a young man who was almost four years older than her.

Calvin always had great charm and charisma, and it wasn't long before both of Shayla's brothers come to believe that Calvin would be good for little sister Shayla. Only time would reveal if this would indeed be the case.

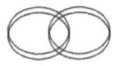

Chapter 5

Chez Marie

The walls boasted red and black velvet wallpaper. The dangling crystals on the small chandeliers that hung just above each table were so beautiful, they reminded Shayla of diamonds.

The round tables had white linen tablecloths, red linen napkins and silver cutlery. Each table had a large candle in the center of it.

The waiters wore tuxedos, and each one carried a white towel folded over his arm and wore a smile that seemed ever present. In the far corner, near the wood-burning fireplace, was a trio of entertainers, with stringed instruments playing soft romantic music.

To Shayla, the music sounded like it was sent directly from Heaven. Indeed, the restaurant named "Chez Marie" was like no place that she had ever seen. But then, she had never dined at a fine French restaurant before—she also had never celebrated a seventeenth birthday before.

Calvin held her hand as they followed the Maitre'D to the table where he promptly removed the reserved sign and lit the candle. It was all Shayla could do to keep from pinching herself to see if this whole thing was really happening. The place was jaw-dropping amazing!

Shayla was accustomed to having a celebration with birthday cake and presents each time she had a birthday, but there had never been anything elegant like this—this was way over the top. Shayla could now understand why Calvin had insisted that they get dressed up for their night out. He had told Shayla that they would be driving the two-hour run into the city. But he didn't tell her where they would be going. Only that they would be celebrating her birthday.

Transportation was much easier since Calvin had bought the car. He had actually bought it from Shayla's brother Wyatt. It was a four-door, 1957 Ford. The color of it was white, however, it had a red hood—and it had its share of dings. Calvin's car was very easy to spot. Most importantly was the fact that, Calvin would not have to be hitchhiking around in sub-zero temperatures anymore. Calvin's car was older but, it was very reliable.

Calvin could clearly see that Shayla was very pleased with his choice of how to celebrate her birthday. And, he also had good reason to be very pleased with himself. He had been saving his money for quite some time with this very special night in mind, and he had managed to accumulate a tidy little sum.

Breaking into Calvin's thought process, came their waiter. He announced that his name was Jean-Claude, and that he would be waiting on them for the evening. Jean-Claude spoke with a barely distinguishable French accent.

Calvin told the waiter that tonight was a very special one, and that he should bring them a bottle of champagne. The fact that Shayla was underage did not occur to either of them. Not that it would have mattered anyway—not that night!

It would be the first time that Shayla ever tasted champagne. She was beginning to realize that she was experiencing many "firsts" with Calvin. And that suited her just perfectly, because after all this time together, she had come to love Calvin very, very much.

Shayla had chosen to wear the white, knee-length sleeveless sheath dress that Calvin had bought for her. With it, she wore yellow gold jewelry and black accessories, including the shoes that Calvin liked so much, the high-heeled ones that laced up around the ankles. Shayla had always liked black and white. She often said that "There is no room for "gray" in my life, everything is either black or white".

Her blonde hair was worn straight down over her shoulders. She had considered piling some of it up on top of her head but decided against it at the last moment. Her hair was so long, that having it on top of her head often gave her a headache. So, she usually wore it loose. Besides, Calvin preferred her hair worn loose around her face.

Calvin looked handsome and trim in his black shirt and trousers. He wore a black and gray striped tie, which complemented his light gray suede sports jacket. In this restaurant the dress code was semi formal. Some of the patrons were even wearing long gowns. Apparently, it was a very popular place; every table was either occupied or had a reserved sign on it.

Gazing at his sweetheart in the light of the candle across the table from him, he felt his heart swell with love for this young woman called Shayla—she had not stolen his heart, he had freely given it to her. And not only his heart, but the whole of his very being.

Calvin had come to realize some time ago, that he would never be complete without her. For when he was not with her, he felt that he was only half, and not whole. Calvin loved Shayla completely and he knew well that she felt the same. They had declared their love to each other many months earlier, and often spoke of the "one-day", when they would marry.

The fact that Shayla was younger was never an issue for Calvin. Now, on this day, Shayla's seventeenth birthday, would be remembered as one of the happiest days of their lives—Calvin would make certain of it!

The entree of filet mignon, the glass of champagne, the birthday cake dessert that Calvin had pre-arranged, the music, everything was fantastic. Shayla felt so very happy, she felt a little guilty that she was blessed with such incredible happiness. She wondered to herself, what had she ever done to deserve such great joy.

The "great joy" she referred to mostly meant Calvin's love and adoration. She expressed this to Calvin as she reached for his hands across the table and whispered, "Thank you my love for such a perfect and memorable birthday". Calvin smiled and replied, "Yes, it will indeed be a perfect, memorable birthday my love".

With the evening nearly spent, Jean-Claude brought the dinner bill in a leather folder and placed it beside Calvin. Shayla thought to herself that Calvin must have saved a long time to afford this evening. She considered offering to pay something towards the evening but thought better of it.

She had long learned that Calvin would not allow her to pay for anything when they were out together. If he had little money, which seemed often to be the case, especially in recent months, then they simply did not buy much.

That didn't matter anyway, what did matter, was that they were together. For the first time in her life, material things seemed to take on less and less meaning for Shayla. Her love for Calvin was overwhelming. Her heart was full!

Calvin excused himself as he went to the counter to pay for the evening. Shayla watched, as Calvin and their waiter, along with the Maitre'D chatted quietly for a moment. They were too far away for her to hear what was being spoken. Shayla thought that perhaps Calvin had found some problem with the bill. She wasn't worried, Calvin would take care of it—he always took care of everything.

Shayla smiled to herself, as she thought of how she had begun taking birth control pills just a couple of months earlier. Although, she still had not told Calvin anything about it, she longed for the time when the two of them would become sexually intimate together. They had discussed it one time, and made the decision, that once they became engaged, then they would become sexually active.

When Calvin returned to the table and sat down, she inquired regarding the discussion with the two staff members. Calvin said that he was speaking to them regarding the musicians. He had told them how much Shayla and he had enjoyed their renditions.

As he said this, he placed his wallet on the table. It was deliberately left open so that Shayla could easily see inside. Calvin said nothing; he just sat there looking at her. It was like he was just waiting for her to say something. She nearly dropped the water glass that she was drinking from, when she saw the wad of cash inside.

Trying not to stare, she looked at Calvin and then at his wallet, then back to Calvin again. Finally, she choked out quietly "Where on earth did all that money come from? There must be a thousand dollars in there". She was not alarmed; she knew that he had not done anything illegal. But she certainly was more than a little curious.

As Calvin moved his chair in closer to the table he quietly said, "Yes, there is fifteen hundred dollars there. Since we are here in the city, I thought that we might do a little shopping tomorrow".

Shayla replied, "But we must drive back home tonight, my mom is expecting me to be home by midnight". Calvin smiled and replied, "No Shayla, your mom is not expecting you home at any time tonight, I told her we would be staying at Jaclyn and Trevor's place—which, isn't true. Because, I have a wonderful Hotel room booked for us for this very special night my love".

Calvin went on to explain, "Your mother is not expecting us back until tomorrow evening. I spoke with her recently, and she is fully aware of what is happening here tonight, or most of what is happening, except for the Hotel part".

Shayla was aware of, and extremely happy about the close relationship that had developed between Calvin and her mom over the previous Months. In fact, there had been such an absolute change in her mom, that Shayla could hardly believe it. Now, when Calvin would come to pick her up, or to have supper, he always got a hug from her mom before Shayla could get to him.

But Shayla could not believe that her mom would ever agree that she could spend the night in the city with Calvin, even if it was to be at Jaclyn's house. Shayla sat there dumfounded.

She said to Calvin, "You told my mother, that you and I were staying in the city overnight? And going shopping tomorrow, and she agreed to this?" Calvin replied, "Yes, yes, and yes". He then picked up his wallet from the table and put it in an inside pocket of his jacket.

Calvin looked lovingly into her beautiful eyes one more time. Those same eyes that were so blue, they had pierced the darkness on the night they had met almost two years earlier. Then he said, "The money in my wallet, I have saved for this special day. It is for you and me to use tomorrow, as we go shopping for a very special gift for you my darling Shayla—a gift that I have decided we ought to choose together—Our Engagement Ring!"

As she opened her mouth to speak, Shayla realized that no sound was coming out. Just then everything around her seemed to be moving in very slow motion. She looked at Calvin; he was smiling bigger than she had ever seen him smile before. She felt totally overwhelmed.

Suddenly, their table was surrounded by the three musicians, and they were softly playing music that Shayla, even amid all the emotions she was experiencing, recognized immediately. It was the song that Calvin had requested for them on the night they met two Years earlier. It was called, "Could I have this dance for the rest of my life?"

At that very moment, Calvin pulled a tiny, flat box from his pocket and handed it to Shayla. As Calvin passed the box to her, he smiled and said that it was about time that he returned this to her. As Shayla removed the small bow from the box, she was filled with bewilderment as to what could possibly be inside.

As Shayla pulled the lid from the box and her eyes filled with tears. Inside, was something of hers that she had not seen nor thought of, since the night she and Calvin had met at her grade nine School dance. She immediately recognized the black velvet ribbon she had worn in her hair the night they first met.

Wiping the joyful tears from her face, Shayla gently pulled the ribbon from the box and held it up, she remembered that night, how Calvin had pulled the ribbon from her hair because he wanted to see it loose around her face, and she remembered how he had told her that "he wished that he could dance with only her for the rest of his life".

Calvin had kept that ribbon all this time and never once mentioned it.

Shayla thought truly, this is my Forever Love!

Suddenly conscious of the musicians surrounding their table, Shayla looked back to Calvin and watched, as he slowly arose from his chair and held out his hand to her. The fact that, this beautiful restaurant had no space designated for dancing didn't matter to Calvin.

Shayla stood and glided easily into his arms, and they began the slow waltz, right there beside their small table. As the music played, Calvin began to whisper the words into her ear one more time, just like on the night they met—"Could I have this dance for the rest of my life, Will you be my partner every night? When we're together, it seems so right, Can I have this dance for the rest of my life?"

Just then, Calvin stopped moving to the music, held her still and stepped back slightly and looked deep into her beautiful blue eyes. Calvin spoke quietly, but apparently loud enough for a few of the other guests to hear, "Shayla,

I love you so very much and I know that you love me. Can I have this dance for the rest of my life?

Will you be my Wife? Will you Marry me?"

Calvin smiled a contented smile, not waiting for an immediate answer, he gently pulled Shayla back close to him, and continued to waltz slowly with the music, which was playing even more softly now. He would await the answer from his love, that he had absolutely no doubt, would be coming very shortly.

He was as certain that he would hear a Yes from Shayla's lips, as he was sure of the breath that he was breathing. She gently buried her head in his shoulder as she began to quietly weep great tears of joy as they very slowly waltzed together, barely moving.

Suddenly, many strange things began to make complete sense to Shayla—it was like a camera that was coming into perfect focus. Calvin's work situation had greatly improved over recent months, with much improved income, however he had seemed to have a constant lack of money these past months. Now Shayla understood that it was because he was saving to buy their engagement ring.

Then, she recalled one afternoon a Month earlier, when Calvin had driven her mom to the store, and they didn't return for more than two hours. Undoubtedly, he was telling her his intentions and asking her blessing upon the marriage.

And then later that week, the three of them went out for dinner, where her mother and Calvin seemed to share an inside secret. Yes, everything made perfect sense now.

Shayla thought to herself, "Everything is in perfect balance, just as it ought to be".

Shayla, trying desperately to regain her composure, realized that the whole restaurant was silent. She could hear only the sound of the soft music, and her own heart beating. There were no dishes or cutlery clanking, there was no talking, no whispering. Just stillness.

All the tables were filled with people, who didn't even know their name, yet they sat captivated by what was happening right before their eyes, they were silent and still. Shayla suddenly realized that in all the commotion and emotion, she had not responded to Calvin's very important question.

It seemed to take all her strength to pull her head away from the safety of his shoulder; Shayla's face was streaked with her tears now. As their song continued to play softly, she stood perfectly still, as did Calvin. She looked up into his wonderful face, the face that she had come to love so completely.

The whole restaurant erupted with applause, when she gave her response to her beloved's question by reciting out loud the third verse of Anne Murray's beautiful song:

"I'll give you this dance, for the rest of my life. I'll be your partner, every night.

When we're together, it seems so right. I'll give you this dance, for the rest of my life".

I "will" marry you. I "will" be your wife!

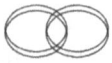

Chapter 6

Lost and Found

From the time Shayla could remember, her two much older Brothers were hunters. Both Harley and Wyatt loved the outdoors, and they loved to hunt small and big game. And they loved to fish. They were not trophy hunters, they hunted and fished for food.

Shayla has a memory from when she was about six years old, when she convinced Harley, her oldest Brother to take her on one such small game hunting expedition with him. He was going out into the woods to check on some traps he had previously set for wild rabbits.

As they came upon one of Harley's rabbit traps, they found that a rabbit had just been caught in the trap, it was alive and appeared uninjured. Of course, Shayla immediately began pleading on behalf of the rabbit. Once her pleading turned to tears, Harley considered his options, and very reluctantly released the rabbit. The rabbit hopped of merrily into the underbrush of the trees.

Chapter 6: Lost and Found

In view of what had just occurred, Harley instinctively knew, that it would be pointless to continue with checking his rabbit traps with little Sister Shayla in tow. So, he decided to call it a day.

That was the first and last time, that Harley ever took Shayla out to check on his rabbit traps.

That would also be the first and last time, that Shayla would ever in her lifetime, have anything whatsoever to do with the hunting of animals.

After that event, Shayla had forever after been extremely opposed to any sort of hunting. Particularly where the use of any sort of traps were to be used. The "little" tolerance she did have for hunting was only if a firearm was to be used, which would result in an instant painless death for the animal in question.

In later Years, Shayla was often heard to say, "God would have a great sense of humor, if he were to ever give me a Husband who is a hunter".

Then, along came Calvin!

What did Calvin love to do? Like her two Brothers, Calvin loved to HUNT!

Shayla couldn't believe it! Here she was, within an inch of being an animal rights activist, and the Man she was in love with—the Man she was now engaged to Marry—was a hunter. Unbelievable!

What were they to do? They did the only thing that they could do, they made a compromise. It was decided between them, that Calvin would hunt small and big game, but never for trophies. And he would never ever use any sort of hunting traps.

He'd use only his rifles or shotgun for shooting. Shayla felt that she'd be able to live with that. This was a huge compromise for them both. They were young, but old enough to realize that good relationships were built upon compromise.

The wedding plans for the following year were starting to formulate. There were so many details to be taken into consideration. Both Calvin and Shayla were living and working in the city, two hours away from Shayla's hometown of Burnt Harbor. Which was where the wedding was to take place.

That fateful long weekend near the end of the hunting season, began with a long list of items to get accomplished during Shayla's three-day visit to Burnt Harbor, where her mom Lydia and herself would spend tireless hours planning and making various decisions regarding the upcoming wedding.

Lydia loved being involved with the planning of her youngest daughter's wedding. And she was delighted to learn, that Shayla had decided to honor her by choosing yellow, which was one of Lydia's favorite colors, for the matron of honor's gown.

Peach would be the color of the bride's maid's gown. Shayla chose this color, because it was a favorite of Calvin's mother, Johanna.

Shayla had come to love Calvin's mom and dad like her own Parents.

Calvin had many siblings. Amongst them were five sisters, three of which were right around Shayla's own age— Sophia, Candace, and Danica were very special to Shayla, and she loved them.

While Shayla was to spend the weekend with her mom, Calvin had made plans with two of his hunting buddies, in his former hometown, for a weekend of moose hunting.

The weekend had been planned several weeks in advance. Everything was all set. Friday was the holiday, so Shayla and Calvin made the two-hour drive from the city to Burnt Harbor on the Thursday evening after work.

Calvin stayed at Lydia's house and enjoyed a nice supper with Shayla and Lydia. Shortly afterwards, Calvin left for the one-hour drive to his Parents house in Morristown. Calvin wanted to make a very early evening of it because, him and his hunting buddies planned to set out very early Friday morning to hunt moose.

They only had the Friday and Saturday to hopefully find an animal. On Sunday afternoon, he would meet up with Shayla, and they'd have supper with his parents, before driving back to the city.

It was nearly noon on Saturday when the phone rang at Lydia's house. Shayla's mom answered her phone. Without the typical pleasantries from the caller, Calvin's father Lesley, immediately asked to speak with Shayla. With a look of concern on her face, Lydia handed the phone over to her daughter. From Lesley's voice on the phone, Lydia felt that something was very wrong. She was right, the news was not good!

Calvin's Dad informed Shayla that, Calvin and Brian had set out from the hunting shack to hunt moose early Friday morning, some thirty hours earlier.

Jeff, (The third hunter) had stayed back at the hunting shack, to keep it heated, because the temperatures had dropped to well below freezing, and he would also prepare the supper meal for the three of them.

Lesley explained that Calvin and Brian had not returned to the shack Friday night. And had still not returned as of ten O'clock that morning (Saturday), which was when Jeff left the shack to return home to report the two men missing.

Jeff had reported that, the two hunters had each taken only a couple of granola bars, and a small jar of water with them when they left the hunting shack. Jeff said that around mid-afternoon Friday, a very thick low-laying fog had suddenly rolled in, and then it had started to snow.

Lesley continued to Shayla that, it was believed that the two hunters, although very experienced, had become lost in the dense fog, and because the snow had covered their tracks, they would have been unable to find their way back to the hunting shack.

Lesley said that it was believed that neither Calvin nor Brian carried a compass. He explained that, due to the extreme cold winter temperatures, the RCMP had now been called, and they would be launching an immediate search and rescue operation.

Shayla had listened to the voice of her future father-in-law speaking to her over the phone, she heard the words, but she was finding it difficult to process exactly what he was saying. A silence fell between Shayla and Calvin's dad. It was as though they had been cut off from the rest of the World.

Then Lesley said, Shayla, are you still there? Finally, she responded and asked him to please repeat exactly what he had previously just told her regarding Calvin's disappearance. Which he immediately did.

This time, Shayla asked her mom also to listen in on the conversation. Shayla then asked Lesley to keep her informed of any new information. He said that he would. He also said she was welcome to come wait for news updates at the family home in Morristown if she would prefer. And then, the two said their goodbyes.

At first, Shayla thought she was in some sort of shock. Then, she began to hear this pounding noise. It felt like her heart was knocking around inside her chest, like a steam engine struggling to start.

Soon after she lay down to rest a little, she realized the noise she was hearing was not coming from her chest at all, but from inside her head, where a migraine headache had taken up residence at the terrible news of Calvin's situation.

A simple ordinary day spent with her mom planning details for her wedding, might never have been remembered as anything significant, were it not for that phone call, the call that could well change the trajectory of her entire future. Her beloved Calvin was now missing! Missing without food, without water, and in temperatures that were well below freezing.

By early Saturday evening, news of the two missing hunters was all over the Radio and TV News. The RCMP Search & Rescue was providing updates to Calvin's family. The news was never good. The news update from the RCMP never seemed to change. It always said that there was no news to report on the two missing moose hunters. RCMP updates came daily, for the next three days.

On the fourth day, the news update changed. The report was very bad. It said that two large holes had been discovered in a half-frozen lake a few miles from the hunting shack. The Search & Rescue Team said it was likely, that the two men fell through the ice while attempting to cross the lake.

They also said, it would be very unlikely that the two men could have survived for this long in the woods, with no food or supplies in such freezing temperatures. The report explained that the rescue team would now be changing from a rescue operation to a recovery operation. In other words, they believed the two hunters had died, either by drowning or exposure.

Shayla was devastated by this news, but she still believed deep in her heart, that Calvin was still alive. She said that she felt the light of his life was still burning.

She also said that she would not give up hope, that she had to believe that Calvin would return to her. She hoped and prayed that he would return to her—and soon!

It was just a few hours after Shayla arrived at the home of Calvin's Parent's that the phone call came. This time, for the first time in five days, the news was good. It was Very good!

The two missing hunters were alive!

They had somehow found their way out to the Highway, they had been picked up by a passing motorist, who had taken them to the local Hospital. They had both been checked out by a doctor and were currently being escorted to their respective homes by the RCMP.

The entire town must have heard the cheers and shouts of rejoicing when that news arrived. Shayla quietly shrugged into her warm parka and went outside to be alone on the veranda with her thoughts. She was no more mindful of the bone chilling wind that was whipping her long hair into a frenzy, than she was of the hot tears streaming down her face—tears of great joy.

Calvin was alive—he was coming home to her. She looked upwards to Heaven and said, Thank You God!

No one ever did understand, how it could possibly be, that the News Media arrived at Calvin's parent's house "before" the RCMP Officer arrived bringing Calvin home. But there they were—one cameraman, ready to capture live footage for his TV reporter; and two newspaper reporters. One local, and one from the city.

They mobbed Calvin the second he emerged from the vehicle, barely able to stand. It was good that the RCMP Officer had the media step back, as Shayla and Calvin's parents needed opportunity to greet him, before the media began asking questions.

Calvin was very, very weak and needed to sit down, he could not speak to reporters while standing outside. So, the news media were all invited inside the house to hear a very brief two or three-minute overview of Calvin's story.

After speaking for just a couple of minutes to the media, Calvin chose the local newspaper reporter, and said that he would give him an exclusive interview the next day at Noon.

The young reporter was thrilled! Calvin suggested to the other reporters, that since they had a very similar experience, they might want to talk with his hunting partner, Brian.

As Calvin shared his harrowing five-day nightmare with Shayla and some of his Family that evening, Shayla sat close beside him on the couch, feeling like she never wanted to move from his side ever again. Calvin held her close, with his arm around her shoulder.

Calvin told of how quickly the thick low-lying fog had rolled in that first day of hunting, preventing him and Brian from identifying landmarks. And at the same time, a freak snowsquall came and covered their tracks, prohibiting them from tracking their way back to the cabin. He said that after the first day, He and Brian had to melt snow for drinking water.

He told how they only had frozen berries, and bark from a certain kind of a tree for food. Brian ate too much bark on day three and became stomach sick for a whole day. This had slowed them down considerably. Calvin shared how they foraged underneath the snow for small pieces of kindling to make a small campfire each night. They would take turns adding kindling to the fire through the night, while the other one slept as close as possible to the fire.

Calvin said, without the fire, they would have frozen to death, as the temperatures remained well below freezing. With no food for nourishment, and such bitter cold temperatures, Calvin said that he knew they wouldn't last too long. He never told Brian that.

He told how at each new daybreak they would begin to walk, hopefully in the right direction. With the fog so thick and unrelenting, Calvin explained they had no landmarks to guide them. He knew they had to just keep on walking! Calvin told about how glad he was that he had recently sharpened his pocketknife because that's what they used to cut kindling.

He also talked about the bic lighter he still carried in his pocket. How now, for the second time in his life, using a bic lighter to light fires for warmth, had likely saved his life. The previous time was years earlier, before he owned a vehicle.

Calvin had been hitch-hiking back home after visiting Shayla. He had to spend a night outside, halfway between the towns where they each lived, in freezing cold temperatures on a snowy Winters night. He was very thankful for his bic lighter on that occasion also. Of course, that was a very different situation altogether. As it was just one night.

Calvin told Shayla, that each time he'd look at his wristwatch to check the time, he would smile at the large S that he had inscribed on the crystal of his watch, a year or so earlier. He said it helped him to keep going.

He finished his story by saying: In the future, he would do one thing differently when hunting:

Besides carrying a pocket-knife and bic lighter, he would also carry a compass!

It could not be known how many kilometers Calvin and Brian walked, during that five-day nightmare.

But this was known for certain: Where the three hunters left their vehicle parked to walk in to the hunting shack, and where the passing motorist stopped and picked Calvin and Brian up at the Highway five days later, was more than twenty-three kilometers!

In the five days of walking up to eight hours each day, the two hunters never saw a moose!

Calvin lost over twenty-five pounds of weight in the five-day ordeal!

Calvin still hunts moose each Year. He "always" carries a compass!!

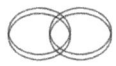

Chapter 7

Here Comes the Bride

Sliding from underneath the covers and sitting up on the edge of the bed at her mom's house, Shayla sat very still and listened to the loud thumping inside her head. Though it didn't happen often, she had always been prone to headaches whenever she had a sleepless night. And, the past two nights, would certainly fit the category of serious sleep deprivation.

Shayla sat there and looked around the bedroom that was so familiar to her. Her and her mom had chosen the blue and yellow paint for the walls and the yellow blinds for the window. The butterflies on the upper half of the walls were Shayla's handiwork. They'd had such a fun time doing all the decorating themselves.

It had been just Shayla and her mom Lydia for the past few years, since Benjamin, Shayla's Dad had died. Of course, Lydia was already accustomed to Shayla not living at home. As she had moved to the city a Year earlier to live with Jaclyn and her Family.

Here she sat, probably for the final time, pondering events of recent years, as well as the events, which led up to this—her Wedding Day!

Calvin, Shayla, and the bridal party had stayed up very late the previous night, doing the finishing touches at the Church. They also carefully secured each of the hand-made rose flowers onto the vehicles that would make up the wedding procession.

The roses were just one of the many weddings preparations Shayla had lovingly and painstakingly completed over the course of the past year. Using the roses and cardboard boxes, she also had made a huge three tier "wedding cake", which was now fastened to the back of Harley's car. It was her brother Harley, who would drive Calvin and herself the one-hour drive from the Church in Burnt Harbor to the venue they had booked in another town, where the reception was being held at the Holiday Inn.

Calvin and Shayla had chosen the Holiday Inn, because of the fifty percent discount allowed to employees. She had been working at the Holiday Inn in the city, as a front desk clerk for the past year. Which qualified her for the discount at any location.

Shayla had quit School halfway through grade twelve and moved to the city where she quickly found that job. The pay wasn't great but, it was full time employment.

Shayla was later heard to make the quote concerning her quitting High School: "There is nothing quite as scary as a bad idea rolling downhill". Shayla had never in her life been accustomed to working for anything so, her immediate future offered up some extremely bitter disappointments.

It took some time before Shayla finished her Grade twelve, and eventually attended College where she obtained a two-year certificate in Psychology. And later, she studied Law for two years, before becoming a Prison Guard for the RCMP. She also became a Provincial Sheriff.

But, in the beginning, it seemed that Shayla didn't think that she would ever need an education. She soon discovered otherwise.

In direct contrast to Shayla, who was raised with everything. Calvin had been raised with virtually nothing that money could buy. As a child, he and his siblings barely had enough food to eat and clothes to wear.

Often, Calvin had worn shoes with cardboard placed inside because, holes had worn through and there was no money to replace them. He was the fifth of ten children born to his Parents Lesley and Johanna. Material things had never been terribly important to him. Their income and possessions were limited, but theirs was a family with an abundance of love and discipline—especially discipline.

Calvin learned at a very early age, that survival is the greatest motivator of all. His parents had taught him some very important principles for life: To be a man of great integrity, to study hard and to work even harder. Calvin learned these lessons well.

Along with the excitement of making plans for this wedding, the lack of funds insured plenty of stressful situations. There was a problem with the wedding invitations. There was a spelling error in one of the names, so the printers had to re-print all one hundred and twenty invitations. There was no additional cost involved however, it did take considerable time to get the new ones printed, and therefore mailing them had been delayed.

The invitations were very important to Shayla and Calvin. They knew exactly what they wanted, and it needed to be done just right. The front of the invitation had two adjoining hands wearing golden wedding bands with the inscription that read: "The two shall become one".

The printing company had one special invitation printed in gold leaf lettering for the wedding couple, which was very special and was greatly appreciated by Shayla & Calvin.

Since Calvin and Shayla had to pay most of the wedding cost themselves, they had to take the path of least resistance where finances were concerned. Besides the ever-present financial crisis that Shayla never quite seemed to elude, were also the quiet comments and whispers that were made regarding their upcoming nuptials.

The wedding date had been set for four months prior to Shayla's eighteenth birthday. Although, no one had ever mentioned it directly to Shayla or Calvin, it seemed to be popular opinion by some family members that, Shayla definitely "had" to be pregnant, for Calvin to marry her so young.

Calvin and Shayla laughed it off and decided to keep the gossip mill running full speed, by not responding to the gossip, and deliberately saying nothing at all regarding children. It worked!

Calvin and Shayla had the last laugh of course, because they had long ago made their plans regarding having children. They intended to wait at least two years after marrying, before trying to become pregnant with the first of only two children, that they planned to have.

About a year after the marriage, Calvin was heard to say to one of his relatives "Boy, Shayla sure has had a long pregnancy, hasn't she?" He told Shayla that he simply could not resist the temptation any longer—he had been wanting to say something about it since before the marriage. But Shayla hadn't wanted him to say anything about it at all. They both had a good laugh over it.

Sitting there on the bed, Shayla's mind snapped back to present reality. The day at hand was Saturday, the Seventeenth day of May, as Shayla willed herself to stand to her feet, the throbbing inside her head seemed to have increased. She made her way across the bedroom to the window and pulled the blind to peer out at the breaking dawn of her wedding day.

She was mortified as she glared at the sight of a thick white fluffy blanket of SNOW! The three decorated wedding cars, including the car with the "wedding cake" attached, were just sitting there, all cleaned and polished, silently awaiting the day's festivities to begin—now, they were covered in snow.

This unexpected snowfall, in the middle of MAY, which was unheard of, threw Shayla into a tailspin. She was beside herself. She didn't know what to do or what to say—she was instantly in tears.

She ran to the phone and called Calvin. The fact that it was only six am, and that everyone would be sleeping, had not occurred to Shayla when she made the call to his parents house. When his mom went to his room and awakened him for the phone call from Shayla, Calvin responded with a big smile, thinking she was phoning to give him an early wedding day greeting.

When he got to the phone Calvin cheerfully said, "Happy wedding day my love". Shayla responded by hollering into the phone "look out the window". Calvin went to the window and realized immediately the purpose of Shayla being so upset. The snow would most definitely be the ruination of all the outside decorating that they had done in preparation for their wedding.

With no more than a few simple well-placed words, Calvin had calmed Shayla. In fact, she felt not only calm, but her headache was gone. Shayla suddenly felt completely rejuvenated, she realized that today she would marry her beloved Calvin, and she would allow absolutely nothing to interfere—not even the weather. She said into the phone, "I must go now. I need to prepare to marry you in seven hours."

As Shayla went back inside her bedroom and closed the door, she gazed at the sight of her wedding gown hanging high up on the wall. She had placed the hanging hook nearly up to the ceiling so that it would not touch the floor.

Shayla and her mom had enjoyed such a wonderful time in the city shopping for the perfect wedding gown. They had both agreed that they had found it, and the fit was perfect—no alterations necessary.

They had also found the perfect dress for her mom. It was a sleeveless full-length gown with beautiful, fuchsia-colored flowers with a sheer long-sleeved duster. Fuchsia was one of Lydia's favorite colors, and she would look so very lovely in her new flowing gown.

Suddenly, Shayla's memory went to her dad, who had passed away when she was just twelve years old. If only things could have been different. If he had been a healthy man, if he had lived and not died! He would be there to walk her down the aisle in just a few hours. If, if, if...

Shayla had very few good memories of her father, as he had been quite sick most of her life. There was one memory of him that she loved to recall. It was a special memory of when she was very young, pre-school years. Her dad would take her up on his knee and sing to her. He had a beautiful singing voice, very powerful. She would always look up into his face when he would reach the very high notes.

As adults, whenever Shayla heard her brother Wyatt sing, it always reminded her of their dad, and those special times sitting on his knee, because Wyatt sounded just like him. Shayla, her parents, and siblings all had musical and singing talent to one degree or another.

But it was Wyatt, who was truly the musically gifted one in Shayla's family. His remarkable singing voice, and competent ability on the guitar brought joy to thousands of people over the years. If he had pursued it in his early years, Wyatt could have been a successful recording artist.

Shayla smiled to herself, when she realized that she didn't recall ever telling her brother just how much his voice reminded her of their dad, and of the wonderful childhood memory it always brought to her each time she heard his fantastic voice.

As Shayla's eye quickly focused on the bedside clock, she thought that it was just about time for her to close the door on memory lane for now. Because the time had come! It was time for her to begin to ready herself to marry her beloved Calvin.

As the hour drew near, all parties made their way to the small United Church in Burnt Harbor to witness the marriage of Calvin and Shayla. The bridal party was small. Calvin's brother Tyler was best man and Shayla's sister Jaclyn served as matron of honor. Shayla's friend Corina and her new husband Allen was bridesmaid and groomsman.

Jaclyn and Corina wore the same design of sheer long-sleeve full-length gown. The only difference in them was the color. Shayla had chosen the pastel colors of yellow for Jaclyn and peach for Corina.

They both carried a small bouquet of roses that complemented those worn in their hair and the color of their gowns. They looked so beautiful.

All things were now ready, and the whole wedding party looked positively stunning as they each took their place at the front of the Church.

The place was silent and the huge double doors at the back of the Church creaked loudly as the ushers slowly pulled them open. The congregation stood to their feet in anticipation of the Bridal march. Burnt Harbor had not had a wedding in over a year so, nearly all the towns people turned out for the event.

Instantly, the piano music changed as the bridal march began. Holding securely onto her bouquet of red roses, and even more securely onto the arm of her oldest brother Harley, they began the long slow walk to the front of the Church. Shayla looked and felt serene, in her full length, sheer sleeved, Victorian-style white wedding gown.

To complete the ensemble, Shayla wore a very long flowing train veil and a tiara, which the hair stylist used to anchor her elegant up-do in place. Her smiling face was partially concealed by the blush veil that covered it.

At first glance of his Bride, Calvin felt his breath catch in his throat. Her loveliness took his breath away. His first thought was that he "couldn't wait to remove the veil and uncover her beautiful face". Halfway down the aisle, Shayla thought she would like to be walking faster. It seemed to be taking a long time to reach Calvin at the front of the Church.

Shayla was happy that she had taken a few moments the previous evening, to admire all the beautiful decorations and flowers that adorned the sanctuary. Because today, she could see no one or nothing but her Calvin—standing there waiting for her to come to him.

Calvin stood there looking more handsome than she had ever seen before. He looked so happy. For himself, and the men in his wedding party, Calvin and Shayla had chosen black trousers, white dinner jackets, white shirts, black cummerbunds, and black bow ties.

The men wore a single rose of the same color as those worn by their female counterparts in their lapels. To compliment his exquisite wedding attire, Calvin wore a smile like the one he had worn more than a year earlier, on the night of his engagement to Shayla.

After exchanging wedding vows and plain golden wedding bands—the kind that have no beginning and no end, Reverend Williams pronounced them to be Mr. and Mrs. Calvin & Shayla Lethbridge. Shayla, holding her bouquet of roses with one hand, she securely tucked her other arm into Calvin's, and the Newlyweds turned to face the congregation in preparation to walk up the aisle.

As they began to take their first steps together as Husband and Wife, the pianist began to play in an up-beat tempo, Anne Murray's country classic song, "Could I have this dance, for the rest of my life.." The song that Calvin had requested for them as a waltz, the first night they met.

The song that Calvin had arranged the trio of musicians to play for them at Chez Marie Restaurant, on the night of their engagement. The song that would forever be, their "special" song.

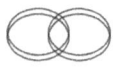

Chapter 8

A Daughter is Born

Shayla became even more hysterical when she overheard Doctor Kaufman whispering to Calvin. She felt that there was something very wrong and she demanded that they tell her what it was. She wanted to know why it was, that after six hours of intense labor pain, her baby was still not born?

A nurse hurried over to Shayla's side and jabbed yet another needle in her arm and one in her back also. She found out later that the needle in her back was to freeze her body from the waist down, because her physical strength had now been completely exhausted from attempting to give birth, and other measures needed to be taken.

Calvin attempted to be calm, as he explained to her that the baby was going to be fine, but that it was stuck in the birth canal. Doctor Kaufman weighed in, that the baby had moved down too far into the birthing position to do a caesarian section, so the only other option was to use suction and forceps to try and dislodge the child. He added that the procedure would have to be done immediately, because the baby was beginning to go into distress.

Shayla could not believe that things had gone so dreadfully wrong. All through her pregnancy she had felt wonderful and had been very healthy. How could things go wrong so suddenly she thought. It had only been a few minutes since receiving the latest needle, but Shayla could feel that it had begun to do its work by dulling the pain.

It was causing her to feel like she was becoming immune to the world around her, the drugs were having a very powerful effect on her. She became more relaxed and was able to lie back on her pillow to rest a little. Calvin had his arms around her shoulders, as much as he was able.

Calvin lifted the blanket a little and began to rub her swollen belly as he had done so many times before. Shayla had always said that she truly believed that the baby knew the feel of his hands, because baby would begin to move around robustly whenever Calvin did this. He smiled into her face and whispered, "these recent months, your belly is like familiar territory but with a different landscape".

Calvin's words made her smile, just a little. His strong hands had always brought great comfort to Shayla, but today nothing seemed to comfort her—only the safe arrival of their baby would bring any real comfort on this day.

While Shayla had never given much thought to God and prayer, she began to silently pray as best she knew how for the safe birth of her unborn child. She prayed, she bargained, she begged, and she pleaded. She didn't tell Calvin anything about her little prayer session.

Shayla also began to recollect all that had transpired over the past while and during her pregnancy. It had been just about two years, since Shayla and Calvin were married on that snowy Saturday afternoon, in the middle of May. A dump of snow saw to it that their wedding day didn't go exactly as planned. But then, nine Months ago, on a sunny Friday afternoon, everything "did" go exactly as planned!

Calvin had left work early, to pick Shayla up in time for the three o'clock Doctor's appointment. The two of them sat anxiously, holding hands in the waiting room of the medical clinic. They sat there waiting their turn to see Doctor Kaufman and to hopefully, have him confirm their suspicions, that Shayla was pregnant.

Sitting there waiting, she looked at the hands on the huge wall clock. It seemed that they moved so very slowly, she felt like they were deliberately taunting her. Shayla became more anxious by the minute, so she stood and paced the floor for a while. Finally, their name was called, and they followed the receptionist to the doctor's office. Shayla recalled thinking to herself, "everything was moving too slowly, even the receptionist seemed to be walking slowly".

At last, they reached her doctor's office at the end of the long corridor. Here, they took the seats offered by the receptionist and then, they waited again. After what seemed like an hour but probably not more than five minutes, her doctor arrived and took a seat behind the large oak desk.

It was not the bone-crushing squeeze that Calvin gave her hand that had caused the tears to flood her eyes. But rather, it was the news from Doctor Kaufman that, the test results were indeed positive. Calvin and Shayla were going to be parents—they were ecstatic!

They had decided that Shayla would stop taking the birth control pills about six months earlier. Each month that went by, they were disappointed to learn that she had not become pregnant. Calvin would just hold her in his arms, smile and say, "That's ok, it just gives us more time to enjoy trying". The doctor had told them that it would likely take a few months being off the pill before Shayla would conceive. He had been correct.

Suddenly, Shayla's walk down memory lane was interrupted by her doctor and two nurses coming back into the delivery room. It was only a very short time thereafter before Amanda Victoria made a dramatic entrance into her new world.

September sixteenth was the date. Which was the exact date that the Doctor had predicted as the expected due date—not something that happens every day! The nurse immediately whisked Shayla's baby out of the room. Neither She nor Calvin got to immediately see their precious baby girl. They both panicked!

Doctor Kaufman spoke very softly as he began to explain that there had been some damage done by the forceps to the baby's right ear. He went on to explain, that the skin holding a baby's ear to the side of the head is so soft and delicate that the grip of the forceps can sometimes cause injury to baby's ear.

He said that, while there was no apparent damage to the front or the internal part of her ear, the entire backside of baby Amanda's ear was separated from her head, and she would need stitches to re-attach it.

Shayla became hysterical once again. Nothing the doctor or Calvin could say to her was bringing any comfort. The nurse who injected yet another needle into Shayla's arm told her that it was to calm her. All Shayla could think of was the pain that her baby girl must be suffering while having her ear stitched back onto her head. Shayla was totally devastated.

The words and phrases the doctor had just spoken took up residence inside her head—those words became like noisy tenants who would not be hushed. Repeatedly, the words played back to her. Nearly an hour went by before baby Amanda was finally brought in and placed in Shayla's arms.

Thankfully, there had been no damage to the inner ear. The nurse showed Calvin and Shayla where they had used eight stitches to re-attach Amanda's tiny ear back unto to her head. To Shayla, it looked very painful.

The very next morning, the surgeon had to replace all the stitches in Amanda's ear. Because somehow, she managed to get her little hand up there and pulling her ear forward, she broke away all the stitches. After the second set of stitches, the nurses kept Amanda laying on her right side. The only problem with that was, her head fell all to one side.

The doctor explained that the inside of a newborn's head is very soft, almost like half-set Jell-O he said. If you don't keep turning the baby from side to side, you end up with a head that is very noticeably lop-sided.

Once Amanda's ear healed, her parents rotated her from side to side when she slept, and her head evened out and was fine. But, for a couple of months in the beginning, her head was definitely a little lop-sided.

A few days after the birth of her baby girl, while still in the hospital, Shayla fell into such a terrible post-partum depression, she thought she was going to die. She had never had a problem with depression. It was something that she had only read about.

It all started when Shayla could no longer have access to her baby. Amanda had developed severe jaundice and had to be placed under special lights in an incubator. She was kept under the lights for eight days.

Shayla became so depressed that she didn't want to see or talk to anyone, including Calvin. The nighttime was the worst. Laying there in that hospital bed, Shayla would try to confront the darkness of the night with thoughts of tranquility and joy. But always, it turned into more of an oppressive nightmare of sorts, it was a terrible time.

Calvin had been offered a good job with an apprenticeship program in Toronto a year after they had been married so, He and Shayla decided to make the move halfway across the Country. Shayla's mother, Lydia took her very first airplane ride when baby Amanda was born. She said, "She just had to see her baby's baby".

Ordinarily, Shayla would have been absolutely delighted to see her mom, but now in such a state of depression she could only pretend to be happy. Shayla didn't even want to get out of bed to walk to the incubator room where baby Amanda was being kept.

The depression had consumed Shayla to such a degree, that she just wanted to lay in the Hospital bed and be left alone to wallow in her misery. It was eleven days after giving birth, before Shayla's depression had stabilized and was able to go home with her precious baby girl.

Finally, Shayla could begin to enjoy some of the pleasures of being a new mom. And it was with great passion and gusto that she began to enjoy her baby Daughter. As did Calvin. It was fourteen days after birth, and three days after being discharged from Hospital, that baby Amanda was diagnosed with severe colic.

For the next three months, Amanda screamed in the morning, she screamed in the afternoon, she screamed in the evening and then she screamed all through the night. She took five-minute catnaps all through the day and night. The rest of the time she hollered!

She only stopped screaming long enough to eat. Her parents gave her the medication the doctor had prescribed, but it did not seem to help at all. It was an absolute blessing to have Shayla's mom there with them to help with little

Amanda. Otherwise, the two of them may well have gone completely insane.

They all took turns walking the floor with the baby. They did this practically twenty-four hours a day for three months. All this happened in a small two-bedroom apartment, while Calvin worked twelve-hour day/night shifts. To say that it was a "challenging time" would be a very great understatement.

Shayla sometimes said, "Life is like a bus route. We map out where we want to go but sometimes, we take a detour or make an unscheduled stop along the way".

Everything does not always go according to plan. The young couple that loved each other so deeply had come to realize that maturity, knowledge and understanding brings responsibility, and in some ways, it limits Ones choices.

As the coming years would unfold, choices and decisions made in their marriage, Shayla and Calvin would experience more than a few detours and unscheduled stops on the bus route of married life together.

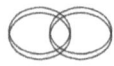

Chapter 9

Perception is Reality

One of Shayla's very favorite authors was Charles Dickens.

He once wrote "Perception is Reality—if one truly believes it to be so, then it may as well be so".

The accuracy of that statement has been debated by some of the world's greatest minds for decades. Shayla had come to fully embrace this concept that, perception is reality. And it was this belief that was helping to erode her four-year old marriage to Calvin.

Over her short time married, Shayla had come to the shattering conclusion that she was likely destined to a life of poverty. To her, this was a very painful reality indeed! To an individual who was raised with essentially everything, this reality was more than a little sobering.

The single biggest mistake Shayla made regarding the deterioration of her marriage, was her decision to not share her concerns and fears with Calvin. She reasoned that she did not want to make him feel in any way inadequate. He had always worked very hard to provide for her and Amanda. And she considered him to be a very excellent husband and father. Besides that, she loved him dearly. And she knew that he loved her.

The first few years of marriage were very good for Shayla. Her and Calvin cared deeply for each other, and they absolutely adored their baby girl. Because of the huge changes that were happening in their lives, those early years afforded Shayla very little time to dwell on all the "material things" that she could not have due to lack of income.

Later, when Shayla was asked the question "When did the dynamics in the marriage change?" She replied very seriously, "I'm not sure, somewhere between the setting of the sun and the rising of the moon, I suppose".

Calvin had just completed the first of a four-year program with a College in Toronto. He knew if he could just see it through, their lives would become much more financially stable. However, Shayla was raised in a manner, which always provided her instant gratification. She seemed unable to see clearly to the time when their financial situation would improve.

Her early life, as a poor little rich girl was coming back to haunt her in a very powerful way. She would sometimes say, "She felt that her past was like a foreign Country to her". She seemed always overwhelmed by the fact that there were never enough finances for her to buy the things she wanted.

Shayla was finding that being an adult with real responsibilities was not so easy. She once said that "Maturity was way over-rated, and that she never wanted to truly grow up because then, she would have to behave in a mature fashion".

Some might say, due to the way she handled certain situations, Shayla would likely "never" have been accused of being overly mature during that particular time in her life. In fact, the opposite was likely the case.

Calvin unlocked the apartment door just as he had done so many times before. It was always around six o'clock by the time he got home from work. Every day, he would do battle with the ever-increasing amount of traffic that always seemed to block up the highway.

The fact that the car was not working properly again, didn't help any. On that one particular Friday evening, something seemed very different to Calvin as he entered the apartment. First, he noticed that the place seemed unusually quiet, and that two-year-old Amanda had not come bounding to the door to greet him, with her usual hugs and kisses.

As he walked into the kitchen and living room area and then ran quickly into the two bedrooms, Calvin felt as though his heart would surely break. Shayla was gone. Amanda was gone. Most everything else was also gone!

There was a single bed and dresser, a TV and table, a foot stool, one plate each of various sizes, one mug, one water glass, one knife, fork and spoon and some cookware that was left out on the counter. There was also a hastily written note sitting on the countertop.

It read, "Dear Calvin, I can't do this anymore. Don't try to contact me. If and when I manage to get myself sorted out, I will contact you. Don't worry, Amanda and I will be fine. I will never love anyone but you, Shayla".

Standing there in the empty apartment, the sound of being alone was deafening in Calvin's ears. He could not believe that Shayla had taken Amanda and left him. He wondered "How could she do such a terrible thing. And, why on earth would she do such a thing?"

Shayla had never once talked with him about any problems that she was having with their marriage. She just up and left! Calvin suddenly remembered something that Shayla had said to him that morning as he was leaving for work. When he kissed her goodbye and said, "have a good day".

She responded not with her usual, "I will, you too", but rather, "don't worry about us, we'll be ok". Calvin thought nothing of it at the time, but now, it's meaning became abundantly clear.

Three weeks passed since Shayla had left. Calvin knew she was staying at her sister Jaclyn's house in Brighten, which was a four-hour drive away.

Jaclyn and Trevor had two Girls, who were more like daughters to Shayla than nieces. Jodi was born two years after Kyra and the two of them were as unique and different in personality as they were in physical appearance.

Also, part of Jaclyn's immediate family was a mutt named Buddy. He was a wonderful little dog that everyone loved. Shayla realized after about a week of living at her sister's home, that her and Buddy shared the exact same taste in shoes. Shayla liked wearing them. Buddy liked chewing them.

Shayla had spent a good deal of time with Jaclyn and her family during the years prior to her and Calvin being married. In fact, both Shayla and Calvin at separate times, had lived at Jaclyn's house for a short time.

Shayla had asked Jaclyn and Trevor not to let on to Calvin that she was staying there with Amanda. But, after numerous phone calls from him, Jaclyn had finally admitted that Amanda and her mom were there, and that they were fine.

Shayla would not take the phone to speak with Calvin. She did, however, allow Amanda to talk with her daddy on the phone whenever he asked. It was never Shayla's intention to hurt Calvin or to keep Amanda from him. She was just in such a state of confusion, that she felt her whole world had gone sideways, and she needed to somehow, get it set upright again.

Her days seemed to drift from one into the other, like a river running into the sea. Shayla was very much the victim in a circumstance. A circumstance for which she was largely responsible.

She knew she loved and wanted to be with Calvin but, at the same time, she also knew that she was no longer satisfied with the lifestyle he was offering her. Which in effect was, barely enough income to supply the basic needs of the family.

Shayla felt that she could not be satisfied with the bare basics; she wanted the extras—at least "some" of the extras. She wanted the stuff that only money could buy. Shayla knew that the world was driven by two main objectives—emotion and greed.

It appeared now, that these two had somehow become her very close companions. She was later heard to say, "never under-estimate a person's capacity for ignorance in the face of greed".

One month after Shayla had moved away, Calvin made the four-hour trip to visit her and Amanda. Shayla had no idea that he was coming. Jaclyn and Trevor knew but said nothing.

Once Calvin arrived and spent some time playing with Amanda, he convinced Shayla to go out for a late dinner with him, so that they could talk. She reluctantly agreed. Amanda stayed home with Auntie Jaclyn while her parents went out.

They went to a quiet family restaurant a few blocks from the house. The place was nearly empty, which suited Shayla and Calvin just fine. Although neither of them had eaten dinner, they were not the least bit hungry. They just ordered coffee, tea, and a muffin, which, they hardly touched.

The end of that evening found both Calvin and Shayla at a place where there simply was nothing left to say. She told him that she had already filed Court documents for a legal separation, and that she intended to divorce him. She told him that although she still loved him dearly, she could not be happy with the kind of lifestyle that he was offering herself and Amanda. She said that she could not live in a constant state of "want".

It was very quiet in the car as they drove back in the direction of Jaclyn and Trevor's house. Calvin seemed to be in some sort of shock. He finally responded by saying, "Shayla, I told you before we became engaged, that I was not, and likely would never be a very wealthy man. I've also told you, that once I finish College and graduate, things will be much easier financially.

Before we married, I promised you that I would work hard to provide a good life for us. I asked you then if you were sure that you could be happy and content with what I could offer you, and you said that, you were sure. It is no longer just you and I involved; we also must consider Amanda".

At that very moment, as though it were scripted, Calvin slowly pulled the car into Jaclyn's driveway and parked. Calvin spoke slowly and quietly when he said, "Shayla, I love you more than anything. I am willing to work on whatever needs help in our marriage. But, if you get out of this vehicle and leave me here right now, I plan to not ask again to reconcile our differences."

He went on to say, "If we are unable to come to at least some sort of understanding for our future together right now, there will be no more opportunities to fix the wrongs. It will be the end of what we had, and it will be the end of all that we could have in the future. Please understand what

I am saying to you". Shayla thought to herself, "If only One could harness the power of parting words".

Without looking at him, or uttering a single word, Shayla simply nodded her head in his direction to indicate that she understood. Then she slowly and purposefully opened the car door, got out and gently closed the door. She stood there for a moment, as her eyes filled and overflowed with hot tears.

She shivered, just a little, as she filled her lungs with the cool night air. Then she stood tall, squared her shoulders, and without looking back at Calvin, she slowly walked towards the house. Walking away from the vehicle, away from her marriage, and away from Calvin—Forever!

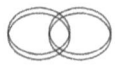

Chapter 10

Order in the Court

The sound of train wheels on the rail track had always been a comforting and soothing sound to Shayla. She had taken the passenger Train many times, to go visit her sister and family in Brighten.

Shayla and little Amanda would take a train ride to visit Jaclyn every few months. They would stay for a week or so, before returning home. Sometimes, Calvin would make the four-hour drive to pick up his family. But most often, Shayla used the train both directions.

On this day, the familiar sound of the rail train only added to Shayla's sadness. As she sat there looking out the side window at the falling rain, she suddenly felt very alone. And she began to feel lonely for her precious daughter Amanda.

At the thought of her young daughter, a tear escaped and slid down her cheek, as she foraged inside her purse for a tissue. Shayla had left her daughter with Auntie Jaclyn in Brighton, while she made the overnight trip.

Chapter 10: Order in the Court

As her train slowed to a crawl on approach to the very busy station in downtown Toronto, Shayla recollected the events of the past few Months. She also considered how it would be to see Calvin again, suspecting that under the circumstances, it would likely not be pleasant. It had been nearly six months since she had packed up and moved herself and Amanda to stay with her sister Jaclyn and her Family.

Shayla was making this train trip to Toronto because the next morning, herself and Calvin were both to appear in Court, to have a legal separation implemented and custody issues dealt with. This had to be set in place before Shayla could proceed further with the divorce she was insisting on.

In the Court documents, Shayla was seeking sole custody of Amanda, and financial support for their daughter as well as for herself. She was offering Calvin full access to Amanda for regular visitation and half of the summer months and holidays.

While living alone for six months, Calvin had come to realize that he was truly miserable without Shayla. Even though, he had previously told her, while sitting in the car that fateful night, that there would be no future opportunity to reconcile beyond that point—Calvin knew, he would still do "anything" to win Shayla back. He desperately wanted his marriage restored.

During his numerous visits to Brighton, he had tried many times to talk with Shayla. Sometimes she would agree to go for a coffee with him. He tried and failed on many occasions, to help her see that they could be much stronger together than separate. Calvin was beginning to realize that he might never reconcile with his estranged wife.

While sitting alone in his empty apartment one evening after a particularly long day at work, Calvin started thinking about all that he and Shayla had shared together. Then he began to think about his little daughter Amanda. He realized within himself, that he simply couldn't be satisfied with the memories of the time he had shared together with his wife and daughter.

Then suddenly, he became angry and told himself that he must not lose his resolve. Calvin was not a fool, he realized that a person's memory can sometimes play tricks on the emotions, and when the two merge together, it can feel like the memories are trying to re-write themselves.

But Calvin would have none of this. If he had to move Heaven and Earth to have his family restored, then by God, that's just what he would do—or he would die trying.

During his visits to Brighton, Calvin always told Shayla that he loved her still. This was the one thing that she did agree with. Shayla told him she also loved him very dearly. That the separation was not about her lack of love for him but rather, her lack of love and understanding of herself. That, for her to be able to sort out her own feelings, she had to be free.

Calvin knew very well that, once Shayla set her mind on something, it would be easier to drink water from a fire hose, than to change her mind. Calvin often phoned and

Chapter 10: Order in the Court

talked to Amanda, but he had stopped visiting once Shayla had him served with the legal documents for a separation. He had said, that visiting there and seeing Shayla was just too painful.

Toronto! Toronto Union station! The voice of the train conductor boomed over the intercom. The sound jolted Shayla back to reality. She found that her face was completely wet from the tears that had spilled from her eyes. She had not even realized that she had been crying. As she searched her purse for more tissues.

She pulled out a handful of pink ones. Again, she began to cry. This time her tears were accompanied by great sobs. The pink tissues were the color of the many hundreds she had used for the flower decorated "wedding cake", that was attached to the back of her and Calvin's wedding car.

She sat there in her seat until all the other passengers had left the train. An older lady, who had been seated near Shayla asked if she was all right—if she could do anything to help. With an attempted smile and a very genuine thank-you, Shayla declined.

Finally, her rail car had emptied, and she arose from her seat and pulled her small travel bag from the over-head compartment. It was nearly five pm and she knew that the rush hour traffic would be at least as thick as the smog, and trying to get a taxi would be a definite challenge.

She had made a reservation at a local hotel near where the Courthouse was located. Her reasoning was, that she would be able to walk to the courthouse in the morning rather than taking another taxi.

Shayla could have arranged to stay the night with one of her relatives or a friend, but she really wanted to be alone with her thoughts. She wanted to be able to "feel the quiet" around her and seriously consider one last time, the consequences of the action she was about to take.

Shayla knew that she had not yet reached the place where she could be certain that, her pending decision was being made from a place of strength rather than a place of weakness. This was a place she knew she needed to reach, and time was no longer on her side. Tomorrow would be too late!

Shayla spent the whole evening inside her hotel room. It was very, very quiet, in fact she found the silence to be so loud that it was deafening. Standing just inside the door and still holding her travel bag, she suddenly thought to herself, "This must surely be the sound of truly being alone". Just as quickly, she realized that it was a sound that she did not care for.

Shayla soon recognized that the ache she was feeling in her stomach was likely because she had not eaten since early morning. She phoned down to room service and had soup, a sandwich and a pot of tea delivered.

Once she ate a little, she did feel better. She had planned to get a shower and go straight to bed to do some thinking. But instead, she settled down into the overstuffed easy chair with a mug of hot tea to do some heavy-duty soul searching.

Shayla allowed her memory to reach back over the six years since her and Calvin had met, and she began to recall many things. How they had loved and adored each other. They had always said that they "choose" to love each other rather, than "fall" in love. Because, if they fell "in" love then, they could also fall "out" of love.

She remembered how she always believed that a real love story has no end—as long as one half of the couple is alive, the love story lives on.

Shayla smiled at the thought of how her and Calvin always said that the best thing to hold on to in life, was "each other".

Then she recalled all the way back to the night they first met—it was such a magical night for them both! With her eyes closed siting in that comfortable chair, she remembered how she noticed him that first night. She recalled what he was wearing. And "how" he chewed his gum. The memory of it was sweet.

She remembered the song that would forever be "their" song. "Could I have this dance for the rest of my life?" She remembered their first kiss. Next, she reminisced about the wonderful evening of their Engagement. She recalled the day they married.

And then she remembered all the events of the day that Amanda was born to them. She was a precious child borne out of love, who would surely grow up to be a very loving person who would contribute to the World around her in a very powerful way.

Shayla knew in her heart that she had not felt whole and complete since she separated from Calvin all these months earlier. She told herself out loud that, she must be "deaf, dumb, blind and stupid, to abandon all that her and Calvin had built together".

Shayla knew that she loved Calvin with all her heart. Maybe he would never be able to provide her with all the material things that she would like but, those were all just "things" that she might learn to live without. She realized that the one thing that no amount of money could buy was the love and devotion that her and Calvin had shared together.

She knew him to be a very hard working determined man, and he "had" promised her that he would work hard to provide a good life for his family. Perhaps she simply had not given it enough time. He did tell her that things would be much easier financially once he graduated College.

Shayla had to make a heart wrenching decision about whether to continue with her present course of action or pick up the phone and call Calvin. She knew that he was just a short distance away and would be there immediately if she asked him to come. As tempting as it sounded, Shayla knew that she was just not ready to make that phone call.

As she looked around the hotel room, she seemed to suddenly need to focus on each little thing in the room—the clock, the lamps, the phone, everything. She felt as though this place, in all its simplicity, in some strange way, had a lesson to teach her. If that were the case, she wanted to learn the lesson well.

Shayla realized at that moment perhaps for the very first time, that there is great perfection in simplicity. She also realized that "peace" is not necessarily a place you "arrive at" but rather, a place found on the "inside". Shayla knew that she had to find that "place" within herself.

Just like that day in the delivery room two years earlier, when the doctor informed her and Calvin of the complications with Amanda's delivery—Shayla had prayed to a God that she did not know, that her baby would be born alive and healthy. Now, Shayla found herself at the foot of another great mountain that seemed too high to climb.

This time, the "life and death" of her marriage was at stake. She closed her eyes and prayed, "If there really is a God out there, please make this crooked road straight, that my marriage may be healed. Please, never let hunger be my guide, and never allow fear to be my master. Help me God, to become all that I can be. First for myself, for my husband and for my precious daughter. Please God, if you are real, I need a miracle. Amen!"

Restful sleep came to Shayla then. She had not known peaceful restful sleep for a very long time—maybe years. Shayla had been curled up in that big comfortable chair, still wearing her travel clothes for nearly four hours, when suddenly, she was awakened by a sound at the hotel room door.

The knock on her door was gentle yet, deliberate. Strangely, the knock sounded somehow familiar—if a knock can be familiar. Shayla quickly glanced at the clock radio on the nightstand. It told her that the time was just past ten pm. She quietly went to the door and looked out through the peephole.

Her knees went weak as she looked out and saw Calvin standing on the other side of her door in the hallway. She could not believe her own eyes so; she peeped out one more time. Her thoughts were instantly interrupted by the sound of his strong, even voice quietly asking her to please allow him to come in. He said all that he was asking for was a few moments of her time.

Shayla, in her state of sleepiness and disbelief, fumbled with the lock and gently opened the door. Calvin looked down at her and offered a little smile. She did not speak; she retreated and took a seat in the chair where she had previously been sleeping—she was speechless!

As there were no other chairs in the room, Calvin sat on the edge of the bed in front of her. He said that "He would not keep her long, that he just needed to say some things before going to Court in the morning".

First, he told her how he had phoned Jaclyn and convinced her to tell him where she was staying. He then told Shayla about how he had wished many times, over recent months that he could hate her—but his love for her always got in the way. He told her how he went looking for other women to fill the void, but each time he met someone, his love for her prevented him from moving forward.

Then Calvin said, I don't really know anything about God. But recently I've been praying and asking God to restore our marriage. Then finally he said, that on the night of their engagement, when he had asked her, Could I have this dance for the rest of my life? I meant for the "rest of my life". Not just until we hit some speed bumps along the way. Calvin said all these things to Shayla and still, she had not uttered a single word. She just sat there on the chair looking at him.

As Calvin slowly stood to his feet in preparation to leave, Shayla also stood. He was totally shocked and amazed when she smiled and said out loud, Surely, there is a God.

When he heard that, Calvin knew in his knower, that the battle for their marriage had been won.

When Shayla walked over to the door and reached up and turned the lock, Calvin quietly whispered, "Thank you God!"

Shayla finally realized beyond any doubt now, that her and Calvin would be able to work through the hard times, always loving each other, and that nothing could stop them now. Shayla had come to understand the true "value" of her marriage and not just the "cost".

Both were in tears as they literally flew into each other's arms. Between great sobs of relief Shayla said: "I give you this dance, for the rest of my life. I'll be your partner, every night. When we're together, it seems so right, I give you this dance, for the rest of my life".

That was a moment that would never be forgotten by either of them—a moment frozen in time!

Regardless of the reconciliation between Shayla and Calvin, the two of them still had to appear in Court at ten am that next morning for the custody hearing. Otherwise, they would have been found in contempt of Court.

As their respective lawyers explained the turn of events to the Judge, both Shayla and Calvin were giddy with delight. The fact that they had talked until dawn and not slept at all, seemed to make no difference to them.

They had learned some very important lessons through all the hurt of recent Months. They realized, sometimes to find true peace and happiness, you must risk un-happiness. To obtain success, you must risk failure. They had also come to recognize that they were much stronger and better together, than apart and separate.

In Court, the judge explained that he would still have to fulfill the requirements of the law and therefore, he was granting sole custody of the "said minor child" to Mrs. Lethbridge and further, that Mr. Lethbridge would be granted full access to the "said minor child". And further, that Mr. Lethbridge would pay to Mrs. Lethbridge a certain amount in support payments on the first day of each month, commencing immediately.

The judge also said, after a period of six months, if Mr. and Mrs. Lethbridge were still co-habituating together in the family home, then the court order would become null and void.

As Calvin and Shayla skipped down the many stone steps of the old Courthouse building together on that sunny Friday morning, they knew that they were now strong enough together to face whatever obstacles life presented.

They also knew that "no dream is more important than the reality from where it is born".

They had indeed risked failure, but more importantly, they had found success!

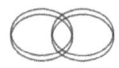

Chapter 11

A Son is Born

Valentine's day came and went with the usual exchange of chocolates, flowers, and Valentine's Day cards. After their reconciliation two years earlier, Calvin and Shayla had determined that they would endeavor to make every day together a special one.

On special occasion "calendar" days, they always tried to make it extra special for each other. The thing they really wanted for each other, was to make every day a special one, like Christmas.

This Valentine's Day, had promised to indeed, be a very extra special day. It was "supposed" to be the day when Shayla would give birth to their second child.

But it was not to be! Little Amanda was four years old and could barely contain her excitement of becoming a big sister.

Amanda didn't want chocolates, valentines, or anything else. Nothing except a baby brother or sister would do. She even offered to help her mom "push the baby out of her tummy".

Another ten days went by. Each day leaving more disappointment in its wake than the previous one. And then finally, it happened!

On February 23rd a short time after getting settled into bed for the night, it finally happened, it was time! Calvin quickly sprang into action. Shayla noticed that he seemed very nervous. It was all very reminiscent of when Amanda was born.

Calvin phoned next door to the neighbor who had been pre-arranged to take care of Amanda. He started the car to warm it up. He phoned the Hospital to say we would be arriving shortly.

Next, he got Amanda up from her bed, wrapped her in a warm blanket and carried her and her pre-packed suitcase along with Marcedes-Angellica, her beloved cabbage patch doll next door to the Randall's house. It seemed to Shayla, that each thing that Calvin did seem to speed up just a little.

By the time she was dressed and ready to leave for the hospital, Calvin was moving extremely fast. It seemed that he was just flying when he carried Shayla's Hospital suitcase down the stairs and ran back up to help her down. Shayla told Calvin to "slow down and take a deep breath".

When she said that, he turned quickly and looked at her. He said, "Oh no! I've forgotten to help you with your breathing. It ought to be me telling you how to breathe".

Shayla smiled and reassured him that, there would be plenty of time for him to assist with her breathing later.

After about four hours of progressive labor in the delivery room, everything stopped!

No more labor pain, no more anything. The nurse said that it might have been a false labor, that Shayla may not have been in true labor at all. The doctor was called at home, while Shayla and Calvin anxiously waited in the delivery room for news on what exactly was happening.

Shayla's thoughts went directly to the day when their precious daughter Amanda was ready to be born, and became lodged in the birth canal, unable to move forward. She spoke this memory out loud to Calvin, and although he too was very concerned regarding the current situation, he tried to reassure Shayla that everything with this delivery would be fine—that this looked like a false alarm.

As Shayla tried to relax, her mind wondered back to when her and Calvin first learned that she was pregnant with their second, and what would be their last child. It had been a very, very happy day.

For a while, they had suspected that Shayla was pregnant. But there's nothing quite like being there and hearing the test results confirmed by your doctor with your own ears.

It was a Wednesday afternoon, and Shayla had taken Amanda to her friend's house. Shayla and a couple other neighborhood at-home moms regularly traded child-care hours. It worked well. If one mom needed to go shopping or had appointments, one of the other two moms was usually available.

On that day, it was Shayla's turn to cash-in a few hours. Calvin had planned to leave work an hour early to pick her up at home. They would go to the doctor and then, they were going out for a special dinner together. A celebration dinner, hopefully!

As they sat waiting in the doctor's office, time once again seemed to stand still. "Waiting" was something that Shayla had never developed much tolerance for. In fact, she disliked waiting so much, that she often said that she could almost use the word hate to describe her disdain for it. However, "hate" was a word that her and Calvin had long decided would never be used in their home.

There were two words that they felt ought to be stricken from the English language: the word hate and the word can't. Calvin and Shayla never allowed those two words to be used. Except to explain "why" the words were not permitted. They agreed, their children would be better off, living in a home void of those negative words.

As their doctor came in through the office door and took his place behind the desk, the huge smile on his face was all that Calvin and Shayla needed to see. They flew into each other's arms, as the doctor confirmed the positive pregnancy test results.

From the beginning of her suspicion of being pregnant, Shayla believed she was carrying a baby boy. She even wrote and dated it, in her diary journal that she believed she was absolutely, positively, having a baby boy.

She greatly wanted to give Calvin a son to carry on his family name. Shayla felt that already having a beautiful daughter, a baby boy would make their joy and family complete.

They had long decided, even before marriage, that they would have only two children. Whether boys or girls, or one of each, there would be just two children.

Shayla's family doctor also recommended that they use the services of an Obstetrician this time around. After the situation that had occurred with Amanda's delivery, they didn't want to take any un-necessary chances during this delivery.

Another decision they had made was that Shayla would be a stay-home mom. They both felt very strongly that their children should have their own mom there to love, nurture and discipline them as they grew and matured. Shayla always said that she would give her two children "very deep roots and help them to grow very strong wings".

The deep roots, so that they would always know who they were, and where they came from. The strong wings, so that they could fly away and always be strong enough to make it back, whenever they needed or wanted to come home.

Her pregnancy had been a joyful one. It was also a very healthy one, as was the case with her first pregnancy. For this, both Shayla and Calvin were extremely thankful.

Suddenly, interrupting Shayla's trip down memory lane, came the deep husky voice of her Obstetrician, Dr. Lowe. As he breezed into the delivery room, he informed Calvin and Shayla that she had indeed experienced a false labor, but since Shayla was already ten days past her due date, he was inclined to induce labor immediately.

As the doctor was still speaking, the nurse quickly went about the business of securing Shayla to the intravenous needle to induce the labor necessary to produce their baby.

Shayla soon realized that having labor induced was nothing at all like going into natural labor, which she had done with Amanda. Induced labor was not a happy occurrence. Shayla experienced very intense bone crushing pain right from the start.

Then after five hours more of the same, Shayla gave one final mighty life-giving push, as she looked up into Calvin's eyes and saw great tears of joy streaming down his face as he whispered to her, we have a son!

It was February twenty-fourth, when Adam Benjamin made his reluctant entrance into the world, and the world was surely forever changed. The light that radiated from his life, was impressive right from the beginning—and has continued throughout his life.

As opposite as could possibly be imagined, was how different Adam was from his big sister Amanda when she was a newborn. Not only in how he looked, but everything about him.

It was as though Adam was celebrating his newfound freedom outside the womb. Whereas for the first few Months of her life, Amanda had seemed to almost reject that very freedom.

But then, in all fairness to their precious Amanda, when she was born, she did have a problem with her tiny ear. Then, an extreme case of yellow jaundice for nearly two weeks, which was directly followed by severe colic for several months.

Whereas Adam was very healthy. He was about three weeks old when, Calvin asked Shayla, "Is it normal that he constantly sleeps, and almost never makes a noise?" Shayla smiled and replied, "Be grateful!"

Amanda so greatly loved her baby brother, and at the ripe old age of four years, she mothered him constantly. When Adam was about two years old, Amanda started school. Missing her so very much, Adam was the saddest little boy each time she would be away. He greatly loved his big sister.

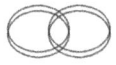

Chapter 12

The God Factor

Shayla had not seen her brother Wyatt and his wife Marsha for over two years—which was just before Adam was born. She had not seen them since they had become "Christians". As she walked through the busy Pearson airport in Toronto, she looked at the overhead inbound flight schedule that had the flight number that her brother had given her. The flight appeared to be arriving on time in about twenty minutes.

Now that Wyatt and Marsha were Christians, Shayla wondered in what way might they be different than before. Her or Calvin hadn't ever spent any time around Christian people so, they didn't know what to expect. It would be interesting having them as house guests for a week.

As a child, Shayla never attended Church. Her parents almost never attended church. The only time she ever heard about God was as a cuss word, or when her father's brother and his wife visited them from the United States every few years. They were Christian Pastors, and everyone was expected to kneel for a time of prayer at some point during their visit.

Calvin on the other hand, did attend Sunday School as a child. Him and his many siblings were sent to Church each Sunday. Although Calvin and his brothers often became side-tracked and didn't always make it to the church. Like Shayla's parents, Calvin's parents almost never attended church.

Shayla and Calvin had already discussed the possibilities of Wyatt & Marsha trying to convert them to Christianity. They thought that Wyatt would likely invite them out to Church with them on Sunday. But Calvin and Shayla had decided that they would have no part of it. They would simply say that they were not interested in hearing anything about religion.

Although they had certainly believed it at the time it happened, Calvin and Shayla had never spoken about the seemingly divine intervention that happened the day baby Amanda was born. When she had become lodged too far down in the birth canal for the doctor to do a cesarian, and too high up for forceps to be safely used. Shayla & Calvin had prayed that day. They prayed that their infant baby who had already gone into distress, would be born alive and healthy.

Their prayers were answered with the safe arrival of baby Amanda, who had nothing more than a minor problem with her outer ear, where the forceps had been used.

And then, on the eve of their Court appearance for a legal separation in preparation for a divorce, they're marriage had been reconciled, by what surely appeared to have been a miracle.

Shayla and Calvin, miles apart, had each prayed to God, asking for His intervention—this time for the life of their marriage.

Again, it appeared that God answered their prayers. They choose to never speak about these things again out loud. However, it felt good to them both, knowing that if things ever got tough, there was a "God" they could call on who seemed to answer prayer. A kind of spiritual security of sorts!

Shayla checked the time; it had been fifteen minutes. She went and checked incoming flights once again—This time the monitor said that the flight would be delayed by twenty minutes. So, she decided that she'd stroll over to where the inbound passengers from the flight would enter. By the time she reached the gate, she heard the announcement of the flight arrival.

Then she saw them, Wyatt and Marsha were at the top of the escalator. It was always very exciting when her family members got together. A good time was always had by all. Surely, Christianity would not have changed her brother and sister-in-law "that" much.

Several days had passed and much to Shayla and Calvin's surprise, Wyatt and Marsha had not once mentioned the fact that they had become Christians. However, Calvin and Shayla could easily see that there was a great change in her brother and his wife.

As Calvin and Shayla discussed the issue one night in the privacy of their bedroom, they determined that as real as the change in Wyatt and Marsha was, it was very difficult to articulate, it was almost like a personality change. They now spoke with greater gentleness in their voice that was not present before. They also appeared to be more loving and attentive to each other than previously.

But the thing that amazed Shayla and Calvin the most was that fact that, Marsha and Wyatt's face looked different. There seemed to be a glow on their face. It was as though their countenance had somehow changed.

Shayla and Calvin decided that since Wyatt wasn't volunteering any information about the changes in his life, then she would simply have to ask him and Marsha about it.

After that evening supper meal was finished, and Amanda and Adam went to their rooms to play, Shayla and Calvin began to ask questions of Wyatt and Marsha about their newfound religion.

Wyatt explained that the reason he had not mentioned anything about it was, because he did not want to be perceived as trying to impose their beliefs upon Shayla and Calvin in their home, in which they were guests. Wyatt went on to say that he would be happy to explain the life transformation that he and Marsha had experienced a year earlier.

The four of them discussed the changes in Wyatt and Marsha's life in detail. Wyatt explained that he and Marsha had experienced a genuine encounter with God. That it really wasn't about religion at all but rather, it was all about relationship.

He said that they had prayed and asked Jesus to come into their hearts. That they had asked Him to forgive any sin in their hearts from the past, and by their confession of faith, through the Holy Spirit, God did exactly that. And that now, they were living a better, more joyful life as a Christian.

Wyatt went on to say that best part was, that they now had complete assurance, that when the time comes for them to die and leave this world, they will get to spend all of eternity in Heaven. Wyatt explained that the Bible says that all people will spend eternity in one of two places—Heaven or Hell, and that we must choose on this side of the grave, which it will be.

Wyatt said that he and Marsha would be going to Church on Sunday morning, and he invited Calvin and Shayla to join them. They said that they would discuss it and consider going.

Go they did! Not only Sunday morning but they enjoyed it so much, they went again that very night. Near the end of the evening service, Shayla and Calvin both came to fully understand the difference they had seen and felt in Wyatt and Marsha over the previous week.

As an altar-call was extended to the congregation for Salvation, Calvin and Shayla made their way to the front of that massively large Church, and it was there, that they both dedicated they lives to Christ—never to be the same again!

Their lives, and generations of lives to come, were forever changed that day—changed by the very hand of God.

Calvin & Shayla with their two young children began to attend that same Church in Brampton, Ontario regularly.

From that time forward, not religion, but a close personal relationship with God became very important in their life. In the immediate years to come, Calvin and Shayla became educated through course study, excellent teaching, and mentorship, and they soon became involved in Church Ministry.

As Years progressed, Shayla and Calvin went on to serve in many areas of Church leadership. Everything from serving on various Church boards to teaching and preaching.

As need arose, they gave leadership to men's ministry, women's ministry, children's ministry, and to youth ministry. But they both found their greatest ministry calling in the counselling and mentoring of struggling couples, families, and individuals, which they did for forty years.

God also gave them great success with a greeter & usher training ministry, which they taught at their own Church, and at various other Churches, as they would be invited.

In the 1980's, Shayla & Calvin had opportunity for the second time, to be part of the massive greeters & ushers teem for a Dr Billy Graham crusade in Toronto.

Following the crusade, all who were in a greeter & usher leadership position at their local Church, were invited to attend a three-day training seminar designed for "effective greeting & ushering" for various sizes of congregations. This was a thank-you, to the local Churches, from the Dr. Billy Graham Evangelistic Association.

Shayla & Calvin attended and were taught many important aspects of that ministry by arguably the most informed instructors in the World on the subject. The first item on the agenda was, "forget everything you "thought" that you knew about greeting & ushering."

For the counselling ministry, Shayla did an eight-week training course also through the Dr Billy Graham Evangelistic Association called: "Counselling—the Christian perspective". She also had a two-year certificate in Psychology.

However, it was basic Bible principles, and a secure loving marriage, that Shayla & Calvin primarily relied upon, during every counseling and mentoring session.

They never advertised their availability as counselors, but through the years, God seemed to always bring their way an abundance of individuals needing assistance. There was often a waiting list.

The counselling ministry, and the greeting & ushering ministry was where Calvin & Shayla concentrated their efforts up to the time of their secular work retirement. Which is when they also retired from the counseling ministry and from the greeting & ushering teaching ministry.

Their children Amanda and Adam both became accomplished musicians, and was involved in the Church music department at a very young age. As teenagers, they were both involved in Church youth leadership.

As adults, Both Amanda and Adam became Missionaries and Church Pastors. They also both married Pastors, and together with their Spouses, became involved in full-time Pastoral ministry, and Missionary work to various Countries.

One might be reminded of the old Randy Travis song, "It's not what you take when you leave this World behind you, it's what you leave behind you when you go."

Shayla & Calvin give All glory to God daily!

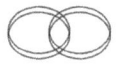

Chapter 13

Promises Kept

Thirty roses make a huge arrangement the young florist said to Calvin, as she eyed him a little suspiciously. Indeed, it certainly does Calvin responded. It is one extra rose than the arrangement I purchased this same time last year.

He smiled and explained that, each year on his wedding anniversary, he has always given his wife Shayla one rose for each year married. He said this year, they were celebrating thirty years married.

The florist smiled and said, "That has to be the most romantic thing I have ever heard". She then began to busy herself with the sizable task of arranging thirty long stemmed red roses, along with greenery and baby's breath in a very large vase.

Calvin had gotten showered and dressed an hour earlier and told Shayla that, he had to go out for a little while. Shayla knew exactly where he was going. He was going to the same place he had gone at that time of year, for the past twenty-nine years—he was going to find a flower shop!

It all had begun on their very first wedding anniversary. During that time, once they paid their few bills and rent, they would be left with so little money, they couldn't even pay attention. It is sometimes said that "necessity is the mother of invention". Calvin and Shayla both believed this to be true. Yet, Calvin desperately wanted to do something special on their first anniversary for his Shayla.

He went and bought one single long-stemmed rose and presented his wife with the humble gift, along with a heartful of lofty promises. Which through the years, he would deliver on, one by one. Because Calvin was a man who kept his word.

That first anniversary day was the beginning of something very beautiful. When Calvin gave Shayla that very first rose, he held her close and said, every year forward, I will present you with a bouquet of roses that will equal the number of our years together as husband and wife.

Throughout the years, it never ever became just a habit that was expected to happen. Calvin always made it very special each year and he always recorded the moment by taking a photo of Shayla holding her bouquet. There would also be photos of the two of them together. If one were to look through their twenty something photo albums, one would find photos of Shayla holding her roses every year around May the Seventeenth.

Calvin also promised her that, every year they would mark their anniversary by doing something special. They did. Every year they had managed to get away alone somewhere. Some years it was only for a night or two, and other years it would be for a couple of weeks. They always went somewhere.

There were many times when they did not have the finances to go out of the Country or even out of Town. So, they would just book a room at a local Hotel in their own city and lock the world away for one or two blissful nights alone away from the regular routine of daily life.

After the near marriage break-up in their fourth year of marriage, they recognized more than ever, the absolute importance of doing special things together. They also maintained one night every week for their "date" night. Shayla's mom or her sister Jaclyn would take care of Amanda and Adam for their little getaways. A babysitter would come to their house for the date nights.

There were numerous times when money was very scarce, when they had only enough to pay the sitter. So, they would go out and sit in a restaurant or a park somewhere and share a treat. They recognized that it really didn't matter "what" they did on their date night but rather, the fact that they had that special time to look forward to each week. That was what really mattered.

The weekly "date" night was one of the sound marriage principles that Calvin and Shayla had passed on to their own two adult children. From the time Amanda & Caleb and Adam & Kerri were married, they also endeavored to implement a "date" night into their own weekly schedules.

Calvin & Shayla also recognized a healthy marriage requires that a couple give each other some "private space". Periodically, Shayla would go off somewhere visiting family, or she would go to the city overnight for some shopping.

Calvin would sometimes retreat to a cabin in the woods that he had helped to build many years earlier. He liked to hunt big game, and Shayla knew that time apart was an important ingredient to a successful marriage. Once they restored their relationship following the marriage breakdown, they seemed to intuitively find an excellent balance in their personal lives and in their marriage.

If you were to ask Calvin and Shayla to name the top five things that have made their marriage a success after thirty years, they would say: Honest, open communication; An amazing sex life; A personal relationship with God; Generous doses of humor; Being respectful to each other— And not necessarily in that order.

Calvin and Shayla have often been asked, how long have you been married? Calvin frequently replied, "We have been on our honeymoon for nearly thirty years, and it just keeps on getting better and better". It made Shayla blush whenever he would say that to people.

Shayla was recently asked the question: "What is the most memorable thing that Calvin has ever done for you?" After pausing, she replied that here were far too many to choose just one.

Then she shared how she loved it that, after all these years, Calvin still calls her his sweetheart. And she particularly appreciated that Calvin would go clean the snow of her vehicle, when she would forget to drive it inside the garage. Shayla smiled and said, Calvin is truly a wonderful husband.

Through all the years, Shayla and Calvin had endeavored to be kind, loving and generous to each other. It made for a more joyful, content life together. Shayla was once heard to say that "Being in love is a state of mind—an act of the will. That there were more important ties that bind people together, other than just emotion. Things like commitment to each other and to God".

Sitting in front of the vanity mirror at the beautiful Banff Springs Hotel, Shayla turned, and looked out the window at the magnificent Rocky Mountains, it was such a fabulous place. They had decided to spend a couple of days there in the mountains, before heading off for their two-week vacation in Florida to celebrate their thirtieth wedding anniversary.

Shayla turning her attention back to the mirror, combed her naturally curly shoulder length hair into place. Up until the time when Adam was born, when she was twenty-four, her hair had always been poker straight. A few months after his birth, she noticed it starting to become wavy. Over the years, it continued to become more wavy until eventually, it actually became curly. She very much enjoyed this change.

Even after thirty years of marriage, two adult married children, and two wonderful Grandchildren, her hair was still the same strawberry blond color that it was the night she and Calvin met. Though, it was now showing definite signs of graying at the temples. She often said, "When her hair became more gray than blond, maybe she would consider coloring it".

Shayla was never concerned, even remotely, by the aging process. In fact, she was always one to embrace the changing seasons of her life. She always encouraged others to do likewise. She sometimes spoke of the tiny lines that had developed on her face. She said those lines are the road map that has gotten me to where I am today, I have earned each one of those lines.

Sitting there awaiting Calvin's return, Shayla smiled to herself, as she recollected all the promises, other than the anniversary flower bouquets, that Calvin had made to her on the day of their first wedding anniversary. He had said, while their beginnings were very humble, he would work and study very hard, and provide well for her and for the two children they had planned to have.

He promised her that one day, he would buy her a beautiful ring with lots of diamonds. That promise came to pass on their tenth wedding anniversary when he presented her with a stunning band containing seventeen diamonds— She was seventeen when they married.

He told her one day, he would buy her the house of her dreams, with lots of bedrooms and bathrooms. That came to pass when they moved from Ontario to Alberta. They bought a magnificent 3500 square foot estate home. It had six bedrooms and three bathrooms on four levels. It was nestled on five acres of professionally landscaped property in a country sub-division, ten minutes from Town.

Calvin promised that one day, he would take her on a cruise ship to a destination of her choosing. That promise was fulfilled on their twentieth wedding anniversary; with a two-week cruise to the Western Caribbean. Calvin followed it up with a three-week cruise to the Eastern Caribbean for their twenty-fifth anniversary.

Shayla & Calvin loved to travel. And were blessed to visit all of Canada's Provinces, and two of the Territories. They also visited about half of the United States of America, plus more than twenty tropical Countries as well.

Calvin's final promise to her on their first anniversary day was, that one day, he would replace the humble solitary ¼ carat diamond in their engagement ring with a much larger gem. That promise had been fulfilled just the previous week, when he picked Shayla's engagement ring up from the local Jeweler.

Calvin had the original diamond and cup replaced with a larger cup to accommodate the stunning new 1.2 carat gem, just in time for their thirtieth anniversary. Shayla looked down at her hand again to admire her original engagement ring with its beautiful new diamond. It truly was a thing of beauty!

She recalled the night that Calvin first proposed to her. And how they went shopping the very next day and found this beautiful engagement ring. The diamond may now be larger, but it meant just as much to her then, as it did now.

Calvin had indeed kept all the promises he'd made to her on their first anniversary day so very long ago. Yes, all those promises, and so many more besides. Calvin was a man who said what he meant and meant what he said. He was "always" true to his word, true to Shayla, and true to his God!

Like his father before him, he had lived his life by a high standard of integrity. Calvin also recognized that one of the greatest lessons in life, was realizing just how much more there was still to be learned. These were the sort of characteristics that Calvin passed on to his own children Amanda and Adam.

Sitting there in the quiet of the hotel room, Shayla checked the time on the clock that sat on the nightstand, she still had about half an hour before Calvin's expected return.

As she looked back into the mirror, at the reflection of the woman looking back at her. She allowed herself entrance into the sacred rooms of her memory, one more time. Her thoughts went straight to the night her and Calvin met nearly thirty-three years earlier, in her little hometown of Burnt Harbor.

She smiled when she remembered the black velvet ribbon that he had removed from her hair on that fateful night. She again looked at her wedding ring finger, and once again admired her beautiful diamond solitaire engagement ring, sitting next to her wedding band. So much had happened in their lives since the day Calvin slipped that ring onto her finger.

Shayla, like her mother, and her grandmother before her, always had a love affair with fine jewelry. In the more recent years of their marriage, Calvin had made certain that Shayla had plenty of fine jewelry.

Calvin and Shayla made sure that their daily life was sprinkled with a good measure of humor. Life always seemed to go along just a little more joyfully with some humor mixed in. They tried always to be respectful of each other. Never in all their years together, had either of them lifted a hand to the other, nor had either of them ever thrown anything in anger.

Shayla smiled at the thought of an incident just a few weeks earlier. Her and Calvin had had a difference of opinion. They seldom quarreled, but on minor issues, they had their own opinions.

On that one occasion, Shayla turned to Calvin and said, "If you believe that, then you are an idiot!" Calvin looked at her and grinned that sheepish grin of his that told her he was "up" to something and replied, "Yeah, well maybe I am an idiot but let's not forget, I am *your* idiot". At which time they both roared with laughter.

Another favorite of Shayla's, was the time she knew that she owed Calvin an apology. So, she stepped up close beside him, offering him her "sweetest" smile, while giving him a loving embrace she said, "Honey, I owe you an apology. I'm really, sorry that "you" are such a bonehead!" By the time they were done laughing, neither one remembered the disagreement.

Shayla glanced at the time on her wristwatch. She was wearing the gold one, with the diamonds encircling the face, it once belonged to her maternal Grandmother. The time was just past six pm. She thought to herself, "Calvin ought to be back any moment now". She quickly opened her small travel jewelry box and removed the yellow gold and ruby necklace, earrings, bracelet and ring set.

This was the final touch of preparation for her special evening out with her beloved Calvin. She thought that it would nicely complement her plain black knee length dress she had chosen to wear. As she fastened the necklace and donned the other ruby accessories, she remembered the joyful occasion for which they had been purchased.

She had bought them to wear for Adam's wedding the previous year. The birthstone of Adam's wife Kerri was ruby. So, Shayla thought it would be a fitting tribute to her new daughter, to wear ruby birthstones to the wedding, then one day, pass the whole set on to Kerri.

A similar purchase had been made several years earlier when their daughter Amanda married her high school sweetheart Caleb. Shayla had purchased a set of beautiful blue sapphires, the set consisted of a pendant, earrings, and ring. The sapphires were not only Amanda's birthstone, but Shayla's as well. Their birthdays were twenty years and two weeks apart. Of course, Amanda would one day receive the sapphire set.

The thought of Amanda and Caleb always brought loving memories of their two children, Jordan and Victoria—Shayla

& Calvin's two Grandchildren. They were born barely two years apart; and they were the absolute sun and moon to Calvin and Shayla.

Their Grandkids, and eventually, many other people, called Shayla & Calvin Nama and Pappy.

The name Nama came to be, because golden-boy Jordan, simply refused to call Shayla "Nana".

He could talk well enough to say "Nama" but he would not say Nana, then he would laugh. After a good deal of time and much effort, everyone relented, and Shayla forever became known as Nama! Of course no one minded, because after all, how often does a first grandchild get to name his grandma?

With a son and a daughter, Amanda and Caleb decided to not have more children. However, Shayla and Calvin knew that before too long, they would likely get to have more grandbabies from Adam and Kerri.

Suddenly, Shayla heard a sound at the hotel room door. Calvin used his key to gain entry and as he walked into the room, Shayla's heart became overwhelmed with love for her husband of thirty years. Not because of the enormous bouquet of roses he was carrying, but simply because of everything that he meant to her.

All the years of history they had shared together—the great, the good, and the less good. Shayla had once told Calvin, that to her, he was like "an island of calm, in a sea of raging waters".

At that moment, seeing him, she felt that she had found her way to the place that she was born to be.

As Calvin crossed the room towards her, he placed the vase of roses on the table beside her. He smiled that wonderful smile at her and said, let's get a couple of photos of you with your roses before we leave for the evening.

After the impromptu photo session, Calvin said, there is just one more thing I'd like to do before we go out for our special anniversary dinner. He dug into his suitcase and produced a small portable cd player. After checking that the battery had not come loose, he placed the unit on the table and pushed the play button.

As he walked slowly towards her, he said, "My sweet Shayla, I love you much more now than the day we married. I want to say thank you for the last thirty years. Thank you for making my life a joyful place. Thank you for sharing my hopes and my dreams. And thank you Shayla for giving life to our amazing children."

He then reached out his hand to her, and she arose from the vanity chair and moved into his loving arms. As he drew her close, it was as though they had become a single heartbeat.

He whispered in her ear "Happy Thirtieth Anniversary my darling, this is the beginning of our next thirty years". Shayla responded, "Happy Thirtieth Anniversary my forever love."

At that very second, the first strains of their wedding song filled the air from the cd player:

"Could I have this dance, for the rest of my life? Will you be my partner, every night? When we're together, it feels so right, can I have this dance for the rest of my life?"

<u>NOT</u> The End!

Thank you for completing *Teenage Bride*.

We would love if you could help by posting a review at your book retailer and on the PageMaster Publishing site. It only takes a minute and it would really help others by giving them an idea of your experience.

Thanks

Sharon Stanford Jacobs at PageMaster Publishing
https://pagemasterpublishing.ca/by/sharon-stanford-jacobs/

To order more copies of this book, find books by other Canadian authors, or make inquiries about publishing your own book, contact PageMaster at:

PageMaster Publication Services Inc.
11340-120 Street, Edmonton, AB T5G 0W5
books@pagemaster.ca
780-425-9303

catalogue and e-commerce store
PageMasterPublishing.ca/Shop

www.ingramcontent.com/pod-product-compliance
Lightning Source LLC
Chambersburg PA
CBHW071509040426
42444CB00008B/1568